Quantitative Methods in Quality Management

A Guide for Practitioners

Edited by
Daniel R. Longo, Sc.D.
The Hospital Research and Educational Trust
of the American Hospital Association

Deborah Bohr, M.P.H.
Division of Quality Control Management
of the American Hospital Association

AHA

AHA books are published
by American Hospital Publishing, Inc.,
an American Hospital Association Company

The views expressed in this publication are strictly those of the authors and do not necessarily represent official positions of the American Hospital Association.

Library of Congress Cataloging-in-Publication Data

Quantitative methods in quality management : a guide for practitioners
/ edited by Daniel R. Longo, Deborah Bohr.
    p.   cm.
    Includes bibliographical references.
    ISBN 1-55648-060-1 (paper)
    1. Medical care—Quality control—Statistical methods.
2. Health facilities—Evaluation—Statistical methods.
I. Longo, Daniel R.   II. Bohr, Deborah.
RA399.A1Q36   1990   90-14398
362.1'068'5—dc20   CIP

Catalog no. 169102

© 1991 by American Hospital Publishing, Inc.,
an American Hospital Association company

Printed in the USA

485 B- pb-87 (10.6)

AHA is a service mark of the American Hospital Association used under license by American Hospital Publishing, Inc.

Text set in Palacio
4M—11/90—0280

Audrey Kaufman, Project Editor
Sophie Yarborough, Editorial Assistant
Marcia Bottoms, Managing Editor
Peggy DuMais, Production Coordinator
Marcia Vecchione and Marcia Kuhr, Designers
Brian Schenk, Books Division Director

Contents

List of Figures

List of Tables

About the Authors and Editors

Francis A. Appel is a director of quality management and medical staff affairs at the University of Maryland Medical System in Baltimore. Mr. Appel has a 20-year career as a quality assurance professional, researcher, educator, consultant, and administrator of hospital quality improvement programs. He is a past president of the Maryland State Association of Quality Assurance Professionals and an active member of the National Association of Quality Assurance Professionals.

Richard J. Bogue, Ph.D., is a research analyst at the Hospital Research and Educational Trust, the research and development affiliate of the American Hospital Association in Chicago. He was previously a senior researcher at Healthcare Intelligence, a marketing research firm specializing in research on drugs and medical supplies. He has had eight years of experience as a university-level instructor and researcher in business communication and organizational and social behavior.

Deborah Bohr, M.P.H., is director of the American Hospital Association's Division of Quality Control Management, which has the primary goal of promoting effective quality, utilization, risk and clinical data management, and infection control practices. She previously worked at Beth Israel and Mount Sinai medical centers in New York City and at the University of California at San Francisco. Ms. Bohr lectures frequently on quality and utilization management and has served on a number of national quality of care advisory committees. She received her master of public health degree from the University of California at Berkeley.

Jennifer Daley, M.D., is an instructor at Harvard Medical School and an associate physician in the Division of General Medicine and Primary Care at Beth Israel Hospital in Boston, where she is the physician consultant to the hospital's utilization review, quality assurance, and case-mix programs. Dr. Daley is a nationally recognized researcher in case-mix and severity adjustment and quality of care measurement.

Carol F. Dye is executive director of Hospital Trustees of New York State in Albany, New York. She is also the author of *The Model Hospital Board Quality Assurance Project, A Study of Trustee Involvement in Quality Assurance Management,* and the editor of *Trustee QA Bulletin.*

Vahe A. Kazandjian, Ph.D., M.P.H., is director of research at the Maryland Hospital Association, Lutherville, Maryland. He also recently became an adjunct assistant professor of epidemiology and preventive medicine at the University of Maryland. An epidemiologist by training, Dr. Kazandjian has participated in a number of national and international population-based studies. In Michigan, he was a planning consultant and research associate for the Sisters of Mercy Health Corporation at Farmington Hills. For the past three years he has also served as assistant director of the Maryland Hospital Association's Quality Indicator Project, which collects, analyzes, and disseminates data regarding proxies of quality of care to more than 300 hospitals nationwide. Dr. Kazandjian has published in national and international journals on small-area analysis, the development of consensus criteria on high-variation surgical procedures, the application of statistical modeling to decision making, and the use of outcome measures in assessing quality of care.

Daniel R. Longo, Sc.D., is president of the Hospital Research and Educational Trust, the research and development affiliate of the American Hospital Association in Chicago. He previously served as vice-president of quality assurance at the Albany-based Hospital Association of New York State, where he developed its first Division of Quality Assurance and began its statewide Quality Initiative. Prior to that, Dr. Longo was assistant director for quality management at Ancilla Systems in Chicago. As director of the multihospital systems project funded by the W. K. Kellogg Foundation at the Joint Commission on Accreditation of Healthcare Organizations in 1982, he developed a modified survey process for multihospital systems, revised standards, and conducted research (from 1984–1986) that was helpful in the establishment and use of its first computerized data base. Just prior to his work with the Joint Commission, Dr. Longo was a consultant to the AHA (1980–1982). Dr. Longo began his career at the National Naval Medical Center in Bethesda, Maryland, where he held various administrative posts, including manager of the 500-bed center's planning services. A frequent presenter at national and international meetings, Dr. Longo is the author of numerous articles and books. He is also a visiting scholar at Northwestern University and a member of the adjunct faculty at Columbia University. Dr. Longo has a master's degree in hospital administration from The George Washington University and a doctorate in health policy and management from Johns Hopkins University.

Jonathan T. Lord, M.D., is the medical quality assurance director at the Anne Arundel Medical Center, a 303-bed community hospital in Annapolis, Maryland. Dr. Lord earned his medical degree from the University of Miami School of Medicine and is board certified in anatomic, clinical, and forensic pathology. He also has earned diplomate status from the American Board of Quality Assurance and Utilization Review Physicians, and he is a member of the American College of Physician Executives and the American Medical Association. Dr. Lord's knowledge of medical staff activities and quality management functions is extensive. He is a consultant physician surveyor for the Joint Commission on Accreditation of Healthcare Organizations and is on the teaching faculties of the Joint Commission, the American Hospital Association, and a number of state hospital associations. He is an active academician, teaching at both the Harvard Medical School's postgraduate programs and the Uniformed Services University of the Health Sciences. Dr. Lord publishes frequently and has coauthored a leading text on quality management as well as numerous chapters for books on quality management, risk management, and ambulatory care.

William A. Schaffer, M.D., F.A.C.P., is director of quality management at Humana, Inc., in Louisville, Kentucky, and assistant clinical professor in the department of medicine at the University of Louisville School of Medicine. Dr. Schaffer was formerly medical director for ambulatory care programs at Humana. Prior to joining Humana, Dr. Schaffer administered hospital and institutional programs, owned and managed a multioffice medical group, and practiced general internal medicine.

Randall K. Spoeri, Ph.D., is a senior corporate statistician for Humana, Inc., in Louisville, Kentucky. He also holds adjunct faculty appointments in the Schools of Business and Medicine at the University of Louisville. He received his master's and doctorate degrees in statistics from Texas A & M University. Previously, Dr. Spoeri served as associate executive director of the American Statistical Association, associate professor of statistics and operations research at the U.S. Naval Academy, and chief of the quantitative methods staff of the User Services Division at the U.S. Bureau of the Census.

Preface

The shape of quality assurance is changing. The traditional case-by-case approach to monitoring care is being enhanced with the complementary use of aggregate data. Although it remains true that it is only within the context of the peer review process that quality can be truly assessed, all participants in the quality management process have come to learn that they cannot manage what they cannot measure. For this simple but compelling reason, all individuals involved in assessing and improving quality must gain an understanding of statistics—the science of measurement. Although quality assurance professionals, like other health care professionals, do not need to know how to perform actual statistical computations, they must become informed consumers of statistics.

This book was developed to serve as an aid in understanding the application of basic quantitative methods to quality management. It does not assume a prior acquaintance with statistics or quantitative concepts and will provide the uninitiated with powerful tools for the analysis of data and the presentation of information. The chapters that follow present the basic concepts of measurement through the use of common examples well known to all quality assurance professionals.

The text is organized into five sections. Section 1 introduces concepts and issues related to the application of quantitative methods to quality measurement, including sampling techniques, data considerations, reliability, validity, sensitivity, and specificity. Using familiar hospital examples, as well as mortality and other outcome data, section 2 addresses the most common statistical tests for comparing provider performance. Using this information in peer review activities and as part of the governing board oversight function is the focus of section 3. Section 4 serves as a programmed learning guide to the basic statistical concepts applicable to the health care environment. Finally, in section 5, a detailed case example illustrates the concepts presented in the book. Although the chapters in this book were designed to be read in sequence, beginning with section 1, readers who wish to review the basic statistical concepts prior to placing them within the overall context of quality measurement and management can begin with section 4.

In the proactive health care institutions of the 1990s, it is essential that those individuals involved in the delivery of high-quality care understand and be comfortable with the process of turning data into information. It is our hope that this book will help them gain that understanding and level of comfort.

Acknowledgments

Editing a book with many authors is never easy. A book on statistical concepts for an audience typically unfamiliar with quantitative methods proved to be a particularly difficult challenge. The editors are indebted to the contributing authors in this volume, not only for their individual contributions, but also for their enthusiasm for the project and their willingness to add sections to their chapters to ensure coverage of important statistical concepts. Without their support and cooperative spirit, this book would not have been possible.

The editors also wish to thank the following people: Audrey Kaufman of American Hospital Publishing, Inc., whose careful review of the content and whose efforts to facilitate completion of the manuscript greatly contributed to this volume; Richard Bogue and Gloria Bazzoli of the Hospital Research and Educational Trust, who reviewed selected chapters; and our spouses, Karen and Jim, who endured endless telephone calls and hours alone so that this book could be written.

Section One

Concepts and Issues in Applying Quantitative Methods

The most basic step in the quality assessment process is the measurement of some characteristic of the structure, process, or outcome of care that is thought to represent quality. Although managers, administrators, and others involved in the quality management process understand and are familiar with this concept, they generally are not equipped with tools of measurement. In this section the authors begin to integrate the concepts of quality management with those of quality measurement. Fundamental issues such as sampling techniques, data definition and accuracy, and validity and reliability are discussed.

Chapter One

From Data to Information: Sampling and Other Considerations

Daniel R. Longo, Sc.D., and Deborah Bohr, M.P.H.

There is a current preoccupation with the use of data among health care professionals who are involved in, and concerned about, quality of care. In an effort to better understand, measure, and monitor their quality assurance (QA) activities and as a result of increased scrutiny of hospital performance by external reviewers, these health care professionals (the medical staff, the administration, QA professionals, and the board of trustees) are raising the following questions: How are comparative rates derived, and how do my institution and its practitioners measure up? How can I interpret data that are being collected by external reviewers about my institution and medical staff? How accurate, valid, and reliable are the data presented? What degree of confidence can I place in these data?

Although these are significant questions, they do not address head-on the main concerns of today's health care institutions: What objective do we want to achieve? Where do we want to go? In order to understand these questions, it is necessary to become familiar with some basic quantitative methods. In the following chapters, the reader will be taken on a journey from data to information. The topics addressed along the way include fundamental concepts and issues in quantitative analysis, the use of data in peer review, and meaningful statistical tools and techniques that make somewhat intimidating information accessible to the uninitiated. Finally, at the conclusion of this journey, a comprehensive example is presented that applies the concepts, tools, and techniques described.

☐ Remolding the Traditional Quality Assurance Model

Traditional QA efforts have focused on an anecdotal, unaggregated case-by-case approach to monitoring care. The result has been a patchwork approach to review, which has led to difficulties in the coordination and integration of findings and to fragmented QA programs overall. Because patient care is multidimensional, many aspects must be monitored in order to arrive at a composite picture of the quality of care.

With the exception of certain sentinel events, such as maternal mortality, most actual or potential quality problems are discernable only in the aggregate and are obscured in any single occurrence. The emphasis on anecdotal, individual case review is therefore shifting to a focus on systematic and comprehensive review of aggregate trend data and the use of quantitative analysis to assist providers in arriving at valid and meaningful conclusions about the quality of patient care.

In addition, monitoring systems are being developed that facilitate coordinated and integrated review methods. Once viewed as discrete and independent data elements, quality, utilization, and risk management data are increasingly being viewed as interrelated and complementary.

Further, the emphasis on principles of continuous quality improvement espoused by Deming and others has proved helpful in refocusing traditional QA efforts. Although it remains for the health care industry to mold the total quality management philosophy to its own unique dimensions and characteristics, this view of quality management supplements the traditional methods of quality assurance, which largely remain valid. The challenge will be in resisting the tendency to abandon what has worked in the traditional QA framework and complementing that framework with appropriate principles of total quality improvement. Although the health services research community is working on developing better measurement tools, such advances will not eliminate the need for accurate and complete documentation, the corrective action of identified problems, the reinforcement of superior care, and the proactive communication of results. However, none of these necessary quality management efforts will achieve quality improvement without a strong foundation of meaningful data in combination with meaningful commitment.

□ Are Data Meaningful?

A nationwide preoccupation with data is evident in the full spectrum of our daily activities. Statistics related to the performance of everything from airline delays to television ratings only further fuel society's interest in, and consumption of, data. This national preoccupation also affects the health care field, where some analysts have naively attempted to simplify the complex interactions of medical and health care delivery to numbers that in and of themselves cannot measure the quality of health care services. With this general caveat in mind, one can say that the use of validated objective data coupled with the actual review of care, usually documented in medical records and subjected to review by peers, is how quality can best be assessed. Although in the past heavy emphasis has been placed on individual chart review, in the future the peer review process must respond by incorporating the use of aggregate data. If data are to be used in the peer review process, the fundamental concern becomes one of whether these data are meaningful. To begin to answer this question, one first needs to become acquainted with two terms—*population* and *sample*.

Population and Sample

In a statistical context, the term *population* has a somewhat different meaning than it does in ordinary speech. In statistical terms a population is not only an aggregation of individuals, it is also an aggregation of objects, events, or observations. Further, because a population generally contains too many individuals, objects, events, or observations to investigate conveniently, a study may be restricted to one or more samples drawn from the population. Correctly drawn and taking into account appropriate assumptions, a sample allows inferences to be made about the population. Although the type of sampling techinque selected may in and of itself ensure that the sample accurately represents the population, two considerations need to be addressed in selecting a sample—the characteristics of the population under study and the location and time period from which the sample must be drawn. For example, the general fertility rate for any given year is determined by dividing the number of live births in a particular area during a particular year by the female population between the ages of 15 and 44 in the same area for the same year.

Probability Sampling Techniques

There are a variety of sampling procedures with which one should become acquainted, including the following:

- Simple random sampling
- Stratified random sampling
- Systematic sampling

These sampling techniques are all broadly referred to by statisticians as *probability sampling techniques*. That is, they all attempt to ensure that the sample to be reviewed and analyzed contains cases that represent the target population—the first principle of data collection.

Simple Random Sampling

Simple random sampling requires the selection of a predetermined number of cases from a list of every possible case in the population. It is based on the idea that each case in the population has an equal probability of being included in the sample. Simple random sampling is also referred to as *true random sampling* and is necessary when dealing with large populations.

Stratified Random Sampling

Stratified random sampling divides a defined population into homogeneous groups, or strata, on the basis of prior knowledge about the population's characteristics. For example, if one were interested in analyzing the length of stay and resource consumption of patients in a medical department and speculated that differences may be associated with the use and availability of prehospital care, one might decide to stratify by payer source, which could include health maintenance organization patients (possibly breaking down this category further into a group practice model as one stratum and an independent practice model as another). Or, if the concern were with patient falls, one might decide to stratify by nursing unit to identify a primary area of concern. Stratification by medication may also be desired to assess the potential adverse effects of a particular sedative.

Systematic Sampling

A third probability sampling technique is systematic sampling. This technique begins with the random selection of one case. A fixed interval is then determined, and thereafter every case that falls at that predetermined interval is selected for inclusion in the sample (for example, every fifth peer review organization physician referral). This process is valid in most situations, assuming that there is no systematic occurrence of a particular type of case.

Although it is important to understand the use of probability sampling techniques in order to understand the variety of quality of care studies and reports released, it is unlikely that such techniques will be used at the institutional level. More likely, nonprobability sampling techniques will be used.

Nonprobability Sampling Techniques

Nonprobability sampling techniques are used when the review and analysis of relatively few cases are all that is required to assist in the assessment of a concern and its probable causes. These techniques are also used when it is neither feasible nor economical to use probability sampling, which requires a number of controls to ensure representativeness.

When a sample is chosen, the goal must always be to select the most representative subset of the population under investigation. One should also assume that the high occurrence of a phenomenon under study, such as a high rate of cesarean sections, is sufficiently uniform (for example, high among all obstetricians in the obstetrics department) and that the most relevant characteristics of the cases are uniform (for example, first births for women aged 36 to 45 years).

Although these techniques permit the selection of a sample that is somewhat typical and may in fact be representative of the population of cases, one must be careful not to make inferences beyond the particular sample. Findings should be supplemented with further analyses and validation through chart review. Further validation studies using different samples are also advisable.

The three most widely used nonprobability sampling techniques are:

- Convenience sampling
- Purposive sampling
- Quota sampling

Convenience Sampling

Convenience, or accidental, sampling refers to the selection of convenient sections of a population, such as all acute myocardial infarctions admitted through the emergency department during the month of January. Although critics cite this as one of the weakest forms of sampling, because it is not known how generalizable the sample is to the population under study, convenience sampling remains one of the most practical and most frequently used techniques, particularly when cause and effect are well established.

Purposive Sampling

In purposive sampling, cases are selected for review for a specific purpose. This technique requires a deliberate effort to obtain representative samples by including presumably typical areas or groups in the sample. For example, if a physician were applying for expanded privileges for a particular procedure, one might review all cases of this type performed by the physician during a period of limited privileges. This example illustrates the need for professional judgment regarding the type and volume of cases required.

Quota Sampling

Quota sampling refers to the selection of a specified number of cases from defined classes. Its name is derived from the practice of assigning population quotas to the type of individuals included in public opinion polls. For example, one might review 10 percent of all ambulatory surgery cases that involved the use of regional anesthesia.

Regardless of the type of sample drawn, probability or nonprobability, and regardless of considerations of statistical significance, there is one important requirement—the findings must be clinically significant and meaningful. When this condition is not met, the data will not be used in a meaningful way. In fact, the use of such data could lead to erroneous conclusions and thus undermine the peer review process.

☐ Other Considerations

Other issues related to data accuracy need to be addressed. First, data definitions (discussed further in chapter 2) must be determined uniformly. For example, when data are collected on hospital readmissions, *readmission* must be defined and collected in a consistent way. Another example relates to the use of the term *death*. For its annual release of mortality data, the Health Care Financing Administration (HCFA) uses deaths within 30 days of discharge; however, hospitals usually review in-hospital deaths. This has serious implications for both the numerator and the denominator that go into the calculation of any rate or percentage, which will be discussed in later chapters.

Once the definition and general data collection methodology have been agreed upon, the human factor needs to be considered. Periodic review of the consistency of data collectors or abstractors and the use of quality control checks or edits in the review process itself should be employed to ensure data accuracy.

In order to effectively deal with data, it is mandatory to have a sound data base. This can be accomplished through the development of a comprehensive quality management information system. Several characteristics of such a system must be taken into account. First, the system must be a comprehensive repository of all quality management information. This includes data related to quality assurance, utilization management, risk management, and infection control. Second, the system should incorporate any data related to credentialing and patient satisfaction. It is necessary initially and then periodically thereafter to conduct audits to determine information gaps between what is *desired* in the data base and what is *actually* available.

Thought must also be given to what form the data may be in. For example, some data may be in the mainframe, some on a personal computer, and some in written reports. Somehow all these data need to be integrated. Even when the full spectrum of quality management activities is not organizationally integrated, the data must be integrated so that they can be presented and used appropriately in the peer review process. The information system must also be accessible. When data cannot be easily retrieved and organized for presentation in a meaningful way, they will not be used.

Data must also be protected. Appropriate safeguards should be in place to ensure that privileged information does not become discoverable. Federal and state laws should be taken into account. In addition, practitioners must feel confident that appropriate precautions are being taken. Finally, the data must be objective.

□ Summary

A basic understanding of quantitative methods and information management systems is now requisite for everyone involved in the assessment of patient care quality. These individuals need to become familiar with how raw data are transformed into information, not only to enhance their own QA programs, but also to determine how external reviewers are judging their performance. Appropriate data collection—the foundation for measuring and ultimately managing quality—is based on a sound understanding of populations and samples and the appropriate selection of a sampling technique. If the importance of uniform data definitions and data quality control cannot be overlooked, neither can the role of adequate management information systems in facilitating meaningful quality review.

Chapter Two

Fundamental Issues in Data Collection and Analysis: Data Definition, Validity, and Reliability

Francis A. Appel

The measurement of a characteristic of an object or an event takes place when the characteristic is assigned in accordance with a particular set of rules. For example, distance is measured when a number is assigned to it that is in accordance with a specific scale of measurement, such as feet or meters. The existence of nominal characteristics of objects, such as a person's gender, can also be measured by the assignment of a number. In this case the rule might specify that 0 is assigned to *male* and 1 to *female*. By measuring objects and events, one creates *data* that can then be examined and analyzed by using statistical techniques.

The most desirable property of data resulting from measurement is *accuracy*. Accuracy means that the unit of measurement is defined with such precision that there is little doubt about the interpretation of the measure. Thus, because there is universal agreement on precisely what a meter is, a length of three meters is generally understood. However, because there is no universal unit of measurement for gender, the values of 0 and 1 will be understood as such only if observers have been informed that that is the rule.

When one moves out of the physical sciences, however, and attempts to measure attributes of some phenomenon in the social and behavioral domain, accurate measurement becomes a problem. When a human characteristic is measured—intelligence, for example—the construct of a test is used to measure responses to questions assumed to represent intelligence. Intelligence is not measured directly. In fact, arguments rage over exactly what intelligence is and, therefore, what an intelligence quotient (IQ) score represents.

The measurement of *quality* presents a similar situation. Quality is measured using some phenomenon that is assumed to represent some aspect of its presence or absence. Thus, the measurement of quality is also indirect. The measures are *screens* or *indicators* of quality. For example, when data are collected using a common quality indicator, such as an unplanned return to the operating room, one measures the occurrence of an event that one infers to be indicative of the quality of care received by a patient who underwent a surgical procedure in the operating room. This event is measured because it is assumed that, at least in some circumstances, an unplanned return to the operating room means that something undesirable or preventable happened, such as a bleed at a suture site or a sponge left in the abdominal cavity. The measure is used as an indicator of an aspect of quality, namely, the occurrence of an untoward intraoperative event. Whether the identification of an unplanned return to the operating room is an accurate measure of quality depends on three properties of the data collection process: (1) the rigorousness of the *definition* of the data elements to be measured, (2) the *reliability* of the measurement, and (3) the *validity* of the measurement.

☐ The Definition of Data

At the risk of explaining the obvious, it can be said that without careful definition of the data elements to be collected, accurate measurement is improbable. Definition is the process of specifying exactly how to identify the event to be measured—exactly what to include and exactly what to exclude. As an illustration, consider again the example of an unplanned return to the operating room. Several definition steps must be addressed before this measure can be useful. What does *unplanned* mean? How is the data collector to know when the event is planned or unplanned? What is intended by the term *operating room?* If an emergency surgical procedure is performed in an intensive care unit because the patient is too critically ill to be moved to the operating room, should this event be counted? What time frame is intended? Are returns within 3 hours included; 24 hours; 6 weeks? A rigorous definition process that addresses these and other questions is necessary if the measure is to measure exactly what it was intended to measure. This step is particularly important when such data are used for comparative purposes. When one attempts to compare measures such as mortality rates or infection rates across practitioners, nursing units, or institutions, the comparison is meaningless unless the measures subject to comparison have been rigorously defined and equally applied, so that the comparison is between "apples and apples."

☐ The Reliability of Data

The reliability of a measure refers to its reproducibility—whether the measure gives the same result when applied repeatedly and by different observers. A yardstick is a reliable measure of the length of a desk because it will provide the same result every time the desk is measured, no matter who is doing the measuring. The same principle applies to the measure of an unplanned return to the operating room. The measure is reliable if (1) the same observer reviews the same case at another time and reaches the same conclusion about whether an unplanned return occurred, (2) the observer applies the measure consistently when reviewing successive cases, and (3) a second observer reaches the same conclusion as the first after reviewing the same case. If a measure is not reliable, it is not accurate, because it does not measure what it was intended to measure. It should be obvious that a careful definition of the measure is essential to achieving reliability.

☐ The Validity of Data

The rigorous definition of a measure and the assurance of reliability are necessary but not sufficient to ensure the accuracy of the data collected. One must also be concerned with the validity of the measure. The validity of a measure is the extent to which it actually measures the characteristic or property one wants it to measure. Measuring a desk with a yardstick to determine that the desk is 60 inches long is valid because the result indicates the desired information. Measuring an unplanned return to the operating room is valid in that it indicates that the event occurred, but as a measure of quality, it is valid only to the extent that it actually indicates something about quality. The fact that one may have carefully defined what this measure means and may have proved its reliability is still of no use if the occurrence of an unplanned return to the operating room does not indicate what one really wants to know. What needs to be known is the *predictive value* of the measure of quality. To what extent does the occurrence or nonoccurrence of an unplanned return to the operating room indicate that an untoward intraoperative event did or did not happen? The measure of quality is analogous to a diagnostic test for the presence or absence of a disease. To understand the validity of a measure of quality, the concepts of sensitivity and specificity need to be explored.

Sensitivity, Specificity, and the Predictive Value of a Measure

Figure 2-1 displays the possible outcomes of the application of a measure of quality to a sample of cases. In the figure the horizontal axis presents the true situation. In the sample of cases, either unquality (the disease) or quality (no disease) occurred. The vertical axis presents the possible results of this test for quality. The test is positive when it tells us that unquality occurred and negative when it reveals that quality occurred.

There are four possible outcomes, represented by four cells: Cell a represents *true positives*; that is, the disease is present and the test reveals its presence. Cell b represents *false positives*; that is, the test shows the disease to be present and is incorrect. Cell c represents *false negatives*; that is, the disease is present but the test does not reveal it. And cell d represents *true negatives*; that is, the disease is absent and the test indicates its absence.

The test is inaccurate to the extent that it results in false positives and false negatives. The consequence of each type of error can be serious. A large number of false positives will lead to the unnecessary examination of cases where no problem occurred. In time, this error could lead to the loss of the data's credibility. A large number of false negatives can be even more serious. Cases with the disease present that need treatment could be missed.

A measure is accurate, then, when its application leads to the detection of the disease when it is present and to the conclusion that the disease is absent when it is truly absent. These measures of the accuracy of a test are called sensitivity and specificity. *Sensitivity* is the proportion of times that the test is positive when the disease is present ($a/a + c$ in figure 2-1). *Specificity* is the proportion of times the test is negative when the disease is truly absent ($d/b + d$ in figure 2-1).

These concepts are illustrated by the data presented in figure 2-2. In this figure hypothetical data are presented that resulted from the screening of 100 patient cases using the measure of "unplanned return to the operating room." For the sake of example, it may be assumed that the phenomenon being measured, namely, an untoward event in the operating room, actually happened in 20 cases. The test correctly identified 15 of these 20 cases, and so its sensitivity is 0.75 (15/20). The test incorrectly identified 10 patients as having the disease who in fact did not. These are the false positives (these patients returned to the operating room but for acceptable reasons). The test correctly identified 70 of the 80 cases where no untoward events occurred, and so its specificity is 0.88. However, the test also missed five cases where untoward events did occur but the patient did not return to the operating room. These are the false negatives. In addition, the test was correct in 15 of the 25 times it was positive. The predictive value of our test is therefore 0.60.

These three measures—a sensitivity of 75 percent, a specificity of 88 percent, and a predictive value of 60 percent—quantify the accuracy of the measure of quality. In this example, the measure is not highly accurate. Because it has a sensitivity of 0.75, it misses 25 percent of the cases we want to know about, and with a predictive value of 0.60, 40 percent of the time it tells us there may be a problem with quality when

Figure 2-1. Sensitivity and Specificity of a Measure

Result of the Measure	Reality		
	Unquality	Quality	Total
Positive (Unquality)	a	b	a + b
Negative (Quality)	c	d	c + d
Total	a + c	b + d	a + b + c + d

a means true positives (cases where the presence of the disease is accurately indicated).
b means false positives (cases where the presence of the disease is falsely indicated).
c means false negatives (cases where the absence of the disease is falsely indicated).
d means true negatives (cases where the absence of the disease is accurately indicated).
Sensitivity equals $a/(a + c)$.
Specificity equals $d/(b + d)$.

Figure 2-2. Hypothetical Results of the Application of a Screening Measure of Quality

Unplanned Return to OR	Untoward Intraoperative Event Occurred		
	Yes	No	Total
Yes	15	10	25
No	5	70	75
Total	20	80	100

Sensitivity = 15/20 = 0.75
Specificity = 70/80 = 0.88

there is none. (In actual use, the accuracy of using "unplanned returns to the operating room" as an indicator of quality may be quite different than what was described in this hypothetical example.)

□ Summary

For data collection to be accurate, the measure creating the data must be rigorously defined. The rules of the measurement must be clearly stated and understood so that everyone using or interpreting the measure knows exactly what is included and what is excluded. A measure is accurate if it is reliable (reproducible) and valid (tells us something about the phenomenon we are interested in). When we measure quality, we use indirect measures; therefore, accuracy is further defined by the sensitivity, specificity, and predictive value of the measure.

Section Two

Concepts of Data Measurement: Preparing for the Use of Statistics

The quality agenda for the 1990s will be dominated by the search for methods to derive comparisons for evaluating provider performance, for both internal quality management purposes and use by external reviewers of patient care. Through the use of common hospital examples, chapter 3 provides a practical discussion of frequently used statistics. Chapter 4 discusses the benefits and limitations of using comparative rates of mortality and other adverse outcomes among hospitals for judging quality of care.

Chapter Three

Statistical Testing: Is What You See Really There?

Vahe Kazandjian, Ph.D., M.P.H.

This chapter explores the benefits of statistical thinking as applied to the daily activities of health care organizations. The chapter's overall objective is to demystify some of the most commonly used, and often misused, methods of data interpretation and to explore the underlying logic and rationale for the choice of a statistic or test. The text does not provide statistical descriptions of formulas, nor does it focus on the mechanics of applying certain tests. Rather, what follows is a practical discussion of the interpretation of frequently used statistics and the rationale for their use in different circumstances.

☐ Proportion Statistics

It is practically impossible to measure and evaluate a hospital's performance without using *rates* and *ratios*. For example, quality assurance (QA) professionals use proportion statistics to depict a reliable and accurate profile of their institution's performance and to facilitate the flow of vital information among QA professionals, physicians, managers, and trustees.

Rates

A rate is a description of the frequency of an observation (for example, of nosocomial infection) within the context of a reference group and the framework of time and place. For example, one could calculate a nosocomial infection rate as a proportion of total infections observed within the hospital, the rate of unanticipated returns to the hospital as a proportion of total discharges, the rate of infections in males aged 30 to 35 years as a proportion of males in all age-groups, and so forth. The denominator of a rate specifies the relevant group to which the numerator is being compared. This process of describing the numerator as a subset of the denominator is called an *adjustment*. In most instances, the numerator of the rate will represent the persons to whom something has happened, and the denominator will represent the persons at risk of having that something happen to them. In other words, the rate will be *based on epidemiological concepts* in analyzing the frequency of an event in a population.

The rate should fulfill the following three epidemiological requirements: placement of the phenomenon within a time frame (temporality), attribution of the observed to the group at risk (risk adjustment), and specification of location. These three requisites (time, person, place) are conceptual in nature.

For example, suppose the rate of tonsillectomy in Community General Hospital was calculated as the following:

$$\frac{\text{Number of Tonsillectomies}}{\text{All Discharges from Community General Hospital}}$$

Although this rate has a denominator, it is clearly inappropriate. In fact, as presented, this rate may be more harmful and misleading than it would be if only the number of tonsillectomies (that is, the numerator) had been reported. One problem is that this rate does not define the denominator in a manner that makes sense relative to the numerator. Tonsillectomies principally are performed on persons ages 18 years and younger. Therefore, the use of all patient discharges in the denominator is inappropriate. Calculated as such, the rate can be influenced by the number of persons in other age-groups, which will be a variable across hospitals and which will render any comparative analysis tentative at best. Thus, the denominator should be changed to include only the number of persons at risk, that is, those persons aged 18 years and younger who have been discharged from Community General Hospital. Another problem with this rate is that the time frame for its calculation is not specified. The rate is unclear and unusable if it is not attributed to a point or period in time and a specific location.

A more relevant rate, which fulfills the three aforementioned epidemiological requirements, would be the following:

$$\frac{\text{Number of Tonsillectomies between January and April 1990}}{\text{Number of Persons Aged 18 Years and Younger in Hospital Service Area}}$$

The last fine-tuning of the construction of a true rate is mechanical—adjustment for the occurrence of the phenomenon in a finite number of persons at risk. The most common adjustment of this type is to calculate the rate of occurrence per 100 persons (the percentage). For example, this would describe the incidence of tonsillectomies in 100 persons aged 18 years and younger. If the rate were small (that is, the phenomenon happened relatively rarely), it might be useful to increase the sample size of the persons at risk in which the incidence of the phenomenon is being calculated. Consequently, instead of a per 100 rate, the unit of analysis may be better defined at a per 1,000 or per 10,000 rate.

Ratios

It is often useful not only to describe the occurrence rate of a phenomenon within a specific time period, but also to compare the present rate to past rates within the same institution. For example, when the rate of cholecystectomy at Community General Hospital for 1990 is compared to the rate of the same procedure for 1988 and 1989, that comparison can be expressed as a ratio. Thus, if the rate of cholecystectomy were 15 percent in 1990 and 10 percent in 1989, the ratio of those two rates (15 divided by 10) would be 1.5, meaning there was a 50 percent increase in the rate of cholecystectomy at this institution between 1989 and 1990. However, the comparison of rates through ratios should be done *only* when necessary and adequate adjustments for the population at risk have been made in the calculation of the rates.

Applications of Proportion Statistics

There are two principal applications of proportion statistics to QA and monitoring activities—*outcome measurement* and *comparison analysis.* Outcome measurement is resurfacing as a screening method of hospital performance (for example, rates of mortality, complications of care, patient satisfaction, and so forth). In the past few years, hospitals have been exposed to a large volume of performance rate statistics, some of which are calculated and disseminated by external agencies, such as the Health Care Financing Administration (HCFA), and others of which are performed by the hospitals themselves. There has been a lot of debate about, and disagreement with, these rates as indicators of hospital performance. The reasons for disagreement are sometimes based on the way a rate was constructed. For example, should the death of a person *after* discharge from hospital A be "credited" to hospital A's statistics without accurate assessment of the cause of death? This concern was raised for the initial HCFA mortality report. (Some common limitations and misuses of rates are discussed in the following section.)

The second, and perhaps more important, application of proportion statistics to quality assurance is in comparison analysis. Hospitals have been searching for ways to compare their own rates to the rates of similar hospitals. This is not an easy task. In the search for comparable indicators, the amount of variability in the setting, environment, providers, and patients makes the use of a rate somewhat more complex than may be apparent. A more complete discussion on the comparability of rates is provided in this chapter in the discussion of regression analysis.

Misuse of Proportion Statistics

It is safe to say that in most situations a rate by itself cannot serve as an indicator of the appropriateness of care. The rate, which is often a rate of a certain outcome of care, cannot represent the *process* of that care. However, it can help raise meaningful questions about the care being given, which can then be incorporated into the peer review process. Thus, by using the rate as a screening tool, a hospital can identify the types of services that warrant further review. When rates among different hospitals are compared, it should be understood that rates can quantify the occurrence of a phenomenon but cannot qualify its appropriateness or desirability.

For example, if Community General Hospital's rate of prostatectomy per 1,000 males aged 65 years and older were 1 and the rate at Anytown General Hospital for a comparable population were 2, one might conclude that the ratio of prostatectomy rates between the two hospitals shows a dramatic twofold difference. However, to draw conclusions about the relative utilization of this procedure across hospitals requires further analysis of the risk factors associated with the patient populations of the two hospitals, the qualifications of the surgeons, the differences in the patients' health care plans, and perhaps the management philosophies of the two hospitals. In summary, proportion statistics are necessary but not sufficient tools for the assessment of the appropriateness of care.

Interpretation of the Numerator and the Denominator

In this section, the numerator and the denominator of a rate are discussed. The degree of accuracy, reliability, and validity in the construction of a rate affects its usefulness. However, it should be stressed that the single most important factor affecting the interpretation of a rate is the user's understanding of the limitations of this statistic and not its degree of accuracy.

The Numerator

The accuracy of the numerator is a prerequisite for the accuracy of the rate. However, the degree of accuracy desired is a function of the objectives behind the use or the application of the rate. In a health care institution (or in the health care industry as a whole), the *accuracy* of observations may sometimes be less important than the *validity* of the interpretation. (See chapter 2 for a discussion of statistical validity.) For example, if 180 tonsillectomies were actually performed at Community General Hospital and the population at risk consisted of 1,000 persons aged 18 years and younger, the true tonsillectomy rate would be 18 percent. If the information system department at that hospital was able to identify only 170 of the 180 procedures, the calculated rate would be reduced to 17 percent. However, the difference between these two rates might not be significant if the purpose of this exercise was to compare the rate at Community General Hospital to that of Anytown General Hospital or any number of other hospitals located in different areas. That is, if the mean tonsillectomy rate at other hospitals was 12 percent, 17 percent and 18 percent both indicate that Community General Hospital's rate is different from the average and that further analysis is needed to ascertain whether the difference between 17 and 12 is statistically significant. If it is, the inability of Community General Hospital to capture the additional 10 tonsillectomies would not affect its decision to investigate the reasons for that difference.

To summarize, it is the validity of the interpretation that is used in the final decision about the specification and measurement of the numerator and not necessarily the interpretation's absolute accuracy.

The Denominator

The preceding discussion on the numerator applies to the denominator as well. The difference is that the denominator might suffer as much from errors of omission as commission. In contrast to the numerator, if the denominator lacks sensitivity (that is, does not identify only the population at risk), it will be representing a sample of persons that may be inappropriate to the rate under study. For example, one cannot include the number of persons aged 65 years and older when calculating the rate of tonsillectomies, and in the case of hysterectomies, one obviously cannot include males in the denominator. Here again, small differences in the denominator may not result in a significant enough rate change to affect clinical, administrative, or policy decision making. Nonetheless, for both the numerator and the denominator, accurate data should always be a primary consideration.

☐ The Mean and Standard Deviation

Rates and ratios are commonly used statistics in hospitals. One application of rates is to construct a mean based on averaging rates from different hospitals for one period of time or averaging the rates in one hospital over a number of time periods. The sample mean is then used as a reference point against which the rates of different hospitals or observations are contrasted and compared.

There are, however, various differences or deviations between the mean of a sample and the rate of each individual hospital, as well as differences across hospital rates. In the case of a sample mean, variability is measured through a specific statistic called the *standard deviation* (SD). The SD is a number that indicates how different the individual hospital rates are from each other and hence how confident one would be in considering the mean rate representative of the hospital's rates. The higher the value of the SD, the higher the variability in the sample and the less representative the mean is of individual hospital rates.

As an example, consider an analysis of hysterectomy rates in two samples (A and B) of five hospitals each. In sample A, the five hysterectomy rates are 3, 5, 6, 8, and 5 per 1,000 women aged 40 to 60 years. The mean hysterectomy rate in this sample is 5.4 and the SD is 1.8. In sample B, the hysterectomy rates are 4, 5, 6, 7, and 5 per 1,000 women aged 40 to 60 years. The mean hysterectomy rate in this sample is also 5.4, but the SD is 1.1. A comparison of the two samples shows that, although the mean rate is the same in both, the sample mean of B is a more reliable representation of the five hospital rates because sample B has fewer *extreme rates* than sample A. The interpretation, then, of high-variability samples is more precarious than it is when the SD is smaller and less variable.

The Importance of Standard Deviation

Knowledge of the SD is of special importance when one is interested in comparing one rate to another. The concept is simple: When there is uniformity, or *low standard deviation,* one has greater confidence in a comparative analysis than when there is high variation, or *high standard deviation.* The concept of standard deviation is critically important to all hospital professionals involved in comparative analysis because interhospital and intrahospital comparisons of outcome rates depend on the degree of variability across hospitals.

In order to evaluate what a rate or proportion means, one must have comparison points or references. Such references could be a statewide mean or average, the average of similar or peer hospitals dispersed around a certain geographical pattern, and so forth. HCFA's mortality data are presented as a range of rates that covers an interval between cutoff points or thresholds considered to be acceptable. A range is determined by the rates of all similar hospitals in an analysis. For example, hospital A's rate may be compared to similar rates in hospitals B, C, and D. If the rate of mortality from pneumonia in B were 1 percent, the rate in C were 5 percent, the rate in D were 11 percent, and the rate in A were 4 percent, A could be presented with the following statistics. Its 4 percent mortality rate would be compared to an interval ranging from perhaps 0 percent to 9 percent, which is the range within which hospital A would be considered *not different* from the group. In other words, if the rate of hospital A were more than the highest cutoff point, that is, 9 percent, that rate would be an *outlier,* or a rate statistically different from the rest of the group. That is the overall logic of an interval. An interval presents a quick method by which absolute outliers (that is, those outside the range of acceptability or confidence) can be identified rapidly.

Interval construction is based primarily on the values of the mean rate and the standard deviation. The standard deviation is used as a gauging statistic for a *cushion around the mean rate.* This cushion is larger or smaller depending on the value of the standard deviation. In particular, when the standard deviation is large, that is, when there is a lot of variation among the sample rates, the cushion will be large and the accuracy of the comparison will suffer. For example, if an interval or a range were expressed as 0 to 99 (as has happened in HCFA's reports when the sample is too small), its usefulness for analysis would be considerably reduced. In contrast, if the range were small, for example, 5 to 23, its usefulness would be considerably enhanced because every rate that is higher than 23 or less than 5 would be an outlier. Thus, a tighter range is a function of less variation among hospitals resulting in a more reliable interpretation.

Standard deviation, therefore, shows how much flexibility is acceptable around a certain fixed number or outcome measure and indicates the points that exist outside that range. Given the generic usefulness of the standard deviation concept, any person conducting an analysis that is intended to compare a single observation to a number of others should consider using it.

☐ Testing the Comparability of Rates and Means

The comparison of a rate to a reference point and of a mean to other group means is the focus of the following discussion. The purpose of any comparison is to determine how different a particular rate is from the "mainstream" rate. Once the absolute values are calculated (for example, Community General Hospital's cesarean section rate for the first six months of 1989 was 22.0 percent; the statewide rate for Anystate, USA, was 24.7 percent), a decision should be made about the most appropriate way to interpret these two numbers. The two most commonly used methods of interpretation are the following:

- Comparing the hospital's rate to an external reference point (for example, statewide mean cesarean section rate) and performing appropriate statistical tests to determine whether the observed differences are significant
- Comparing the hospital's current rate to its past rates to determine whether there is a pattern that could help explain any difference between the hospital's current rate and the statewide mean rate

The most desirable approach is to use both methods, that is, to initiate the comparison to an external reference point (for example, statewide rate) and to construct the hospital's profile using past trends. In both of these approaches there is a single important underlying question that must be answered: How can an *observed* rate be compared to an *expected* rate? In the previous example, the observed rate is the cesarean section rate at Community General Hospital, and the expected rate could be either the statewide mean or the past rates for this procedure at Community General Hospital.

The test of comparability of observed and expected rates can be achieved through either of two statistical methods: a chi-square test or a regression analysis. The correct application, as well as misapplication, of these two methods is discussed next. (See table 3-1 for a summary of what these methods can and cannot do.)

Chi-Square Test

The chi-square test compares the frequency of an observed occurrence with the frequency of an expected occurrence (based on previous as well as concurrent experience) and tests whether the observed and expected occurrences are or are not different (statistical significance). However, it compares *counts and not rates or ratios*. For example, if the statewide annual mortality rate from pneumonia was known, the chi-square test could not be used to compare the rate of hospital A to the statewide rate. But, if the comparison was between 15 tonsillectomies at Community General Hospital and 24 tonsillectomies at a competitor hospital, the chi-square test would be a statistically correct method to use to compare the two numbers. Such a comparison, however, is conceptually meaningless because it is not a rate and, depending on the denominator, the difference between 15 and 24 may change.

The chi-square test is frequently encountered in health services research because of its simplicity. First, small numbers can be used. For example, using only two numbers—the observed and the expected values—it is possible to decide whether the observation is significantly different. Second, a chi-square test can be performed on a small number of observations in both the observed and the expected. For example, one can compare the difference between six as the observed and eight as the expected. Often, statistical tests require much larger sample sizes (30 observations or more). Finally, and perhaps most important, the chi-square test is familiar to physicians because it is frequently used in medical literature, where it is employed to compare the effectiveness of different treatment modalities. For example, group A received drug Z and group B received a placebo. How did the same disease progress in both groups

Table 3-1. Summary of the Capabilities of the Chi-Square Test and Regression Analysis

Method	Can Do	Cannot Do
Chi-square test	• Detect differences among absolute counts of events (for example, 50 T&As, 64 prostatectomies, and so on)	• Compare measured quantities (that is, a chi-square test should not be applied to compare rates, proportions, percentages, and so on)
Regression analysis	• Assess the amount of variation in the dependent variable explanation by each independent variable	• Ascertain the relevance of independent variables to the phenomenon under study; can only assess their degree of association
	• Predict the changes in the independent variable when one or more of the independent variables are changed	• Function as a modeling tool, except when the model is statistically significant

A and B given the two treatment modalities? In such a case, the outcome of the treatments is expressed as counts and not as rates or ratios. Thus a chi-square test is appropriate.

Regression Analysis

Regression analysis provides an assessment of the effect of numerous factors on the phenomenon under study. Thus, it is called a *multifactorial* analysis.

Regression analysis has the following characteristics:

- It tests the means of multiple groups.
- It quantifies and controls intervariable effects.

For example, if the phenomenon under study was the difference in mortality rates between two hospitals in Anystate, potential explanatory factors of that difference could include patient risk in each hospital, the geographic location of each hospital, the number of board-certified physicians in each hospital, the proportion of older patients in each hospital, and so forth. In regression analysis, these explanatory factors are called *independent variables* and the phenomenon under study (mortality rates) is the *dependent variable*. Simply put, regression analysis helps to assess the type of effect each independent variable has on the dependent variable (for example, the extent to which patient risk, geographic location, and so forth affect inpatient mortality). In addition, regression analysis helps to predict what could happen if the value of an independent variable were changed. That is why regression analysis is used in *predictive model* generation, such as the approach used by HCFA in predicting a hospital's expected mortality range, given a select set of that hospital's characteristics (independent variables).

Context of Use

Outcome measures of care are increasingly used to indicate the nature of the relationship between the process of care and the resulting modification in patients' health status. The underlying assumption in the search for the association between process and outcome is that the process of care in some way has an effect on or modifies a patient's health status. In many situations, that assumption has been challenged due to the natural course of a disease. However, for purposes of this discussion, it will be assumed that an association does exist between the process of care and its outcome.

In describing a phenomenon such as outcome of care, variation in outcome over time, place, person, and provider of care is anticipated. The key issue is one of relativity. That is, given the situation, or relative to the environment within which that phenomenon took place, the actual outcomes will vary. The environment can be considered a "bundle of factors." These factors have various degrees of influence on the phenomenon being examined, namely, the outcome of care. A reasonable method is required to allow for the identification of the most relevant factors that influence the outcome of care and an assessment of their degree of influence on this outcome. The search for those factors and the strength of their association with the phenomenon under study is a stepwise process—a process whereby additional knowledge or understanding will be added on to preceding pieces of knowledge about the interrelationships of those factors.

Identification of the Factors

The conceptual framework for regression analysis involves identifying the factors assumed to have some association with the outcome being examined. It seems reasonable to start by identifying factors that other investigators have found useful in explaining similar phenomena. These factors can be found in health services research and in the medical literature. Often, however, a particular environment will not be exactly the same as those that served as a context for previous research. Thus, additional factors could be added that might be more specific to that particular environment. A group of experts in the field might also be gathered to provide a laundry list of potential explanatory factors, that is, factors believed to explain a certain amount of the variation in the phenomenon. This final list should be comprehensive without including factors that seem totally unreasonable.

Example of Regression Analysis Application

Community General Hospital applied the concepts of regression analysis in an attempt to understand and explain a particular outcome phenomenon. Community General Hospital's cesarean section rate had been consistently higher than the rates of two of its competitor hospitals in Anytown, as well as higher than the statewide rate for the past four years. The QA director at the hospital was instrumental in identifying the comparative rates and submitted a number of recommendations to the chairperson of the QA committee, the medical director, and the hospital's administrators. After the fourth report was submitted, the chairperson of the QA committee (following the recommendations of the hospital's chief executive officer [CEO] and the medical director) asked the QA director to perform a quantitative analysis to determine the reasons for the consistently higher cesarean section rates.

A fair amount of national research has been done on the reasons for differences in cesarean section rates. These studies suggest that patient characteristics, and the experience, training, and philosophy of physicians may be associated with the frequency of cesarean sections. To assess the relevance of these factors, Community General Hospital formed an advisory committee that included (in addition to the chairperson of the obstetrics and gynecology department) the medical director, the CEO, the QA director, and, as a consultant, a researcher from Whygoto University. Their charge was (1) to identify the factors believed to affect and explain the differences in cesarean section rates and (2) to quantify a discrete set of variables that measure these factors.

The advisory committee's recommendations were the following:

- Patient characteristics, physician characteristics, and hospital policies are relevant factors and should be considered. In addition, given the physician and hospital reimbursement methods in this state, the analysis should include variables describing payment characteristics.
- The factors and variables should be analyzed both individually and as a group. The rationale for this is the expected *interdependence* among the set of factors. Consequently, the effect of each factor on the cesarean section rate is a function of, and is dependent on, how the other factors interplay.

- Although the committee's analysis would at best describe a *profile* of associations among a set of factors and the rate of cesarean sections over the past four years, its findings could not be used to explain why a *particular patient* had a cesarean section. The latter determination could be accomplished only within the context of peer review.

The preceding example shows the potential uses of an analytic method that can tease out and describe the relative effects of a set of variables on aspects of hospital care (in this case, the frequency with which cesarean sections are performed).

Understanding the Regression Equation

How is the predictive model expressed? Regression analysis can result in the following three types of statistics:

- *A descriptor (explanation) of how much of the variation in the dependent variable the model was able to explain.* In other words, it can provide an indication of how successful the set of independent variables was in capturing or explaining differences in the dependent variable (for example, cesarean section rates). This is the explanatory power of the regression model. In the equation, the explanatory power is expressed by a percentage through what is called the R_2 *statistic.* For example, an R_2 of 0.15 means that the set of independent variables collectively explained 15 percent of the variation in the dependent variable. Perhaps more important is the observation that 85 percent ($1.00 - 0.15 = 0.85$, or 85 percent) variability is left unexplained.
- *A prediction of what will happen to the value of the dependent variable when all or some of the independent variables change.* These predictive values are derived through weights that accompany each independent variable in the regression equation. These weights are called *regression coefficients,* and their value shows the direction (negative or positive) and the amount of effect each independent variable has on the dependent variable.
- *The F statistic, which is a multivariable test that provides an assessment of the statistical significance of the regression equation.* In this sense, the *F* statistic is equivalent to a series of *t* statistics, which compare the means of pairs of factors. The *F* statistic compares the means of many groups and is therefore called a multifactorial test of means. In other words, it will demonstrate that both the predictive values of the coefficients in each independent variable and the percent of the variation explained by those independent variables are not due to chance. That is what any statistical test of significance does. When the *F* statistic is not statistically significant, the regression equation is not a good model for capturing the important factors associated with the dependent variables. The model should then be replaced by a new one (that is, the set of variables modified) until significance is achieved.

Because the objective of this discussion is to provide an understanding of the conceptual framework behind this analytic model, the more technical aspects of regression analysis are not presented. However, there is one additional aspect of regression analysis that deserves special attention—the difference between a causal relationship and an association.

Causality and Correlation

Regression analysis *cannot* determine causality. However, it can partially describe the independent and collective relationship of a number of variables hypothesized for association with the phenomenon under study. Specifically, the regression equation provides a measure of association (coefficients) for each independent variable that indicates how much and in what direction the phenomenon under study (dependent variable) is expected to vary, given a unit change in each independent variable. In addition, the regression equation provides a global or collective measure of the strengths of all the independent variables in explanations of the dependent variable. Finally, tests of statistical significance are provided to help the interpreter ascertain the following:

- Whether the measures of association that are derived relate to associations (or correlations) between independent and dependent variables
- Whether the results of the analysis are simply due to chance or are artifacts of the design

It is critical, therefore, to recognize that the interpretation of a regression analysis should be careful and tentative, even when the associations are found to be real (that is, statistically significant).

Regression analysis is a useful statistical method for discerning and assessing the types and strengths of associations between a set of independent variables and a dependent variable. The choice of independent variables is a function of the amount of knowledge available, as well as the availability of data necessary to quantify the dependent variable. A single regression equation cannot encompass all aspects that can affect the variability of the dependent variable, the strengths and even the direction of some independent variables may change across regression equations as the model is changed. Thus, the validity of the relationship between independent and dependent variables can be assured only if comparable results occur across several studies and regression models. Meanwhile, the stepwise method of inquiry that constitutes the decision-making process (the conceptual framework) of any regression analysis can become a very useful approach to understanding which factors are associated with an outcome of care and to what extent.

□ Summary

The principal objective of this chapter was to familiarize hospital professionals with the most useful analytic methods in the study of hospital performance. To avoid inadequate interpretations, the following should be kept in mind:

- Absolute values of numbers cannot serve as the only basis for comparison. In fact, the use of unadjusted statistics should be avoided as much as possible. Even when adjustments are made, numbers should not be expected to explain, but only to quantify the issues to be addressed.
- Statistical tests for a comparison of values are necessary but not sufficient tools for interpreting findings of a comparative analysis. Assessing a hospital's performance (through rates or other statistics) should encompass the consideration of numerous factors in addition to these statistical tests.
- Knowledge of, and proficiency in, statistical jargon and the mechanics of tests are not necessary for understanding a methodology. Common sense coupled with an understanding of the concepts underlying the methodology are often sufficient. If the proposed methodology or analysis "does not make sense," one should not assume that it is "too technical." Statistical methods are simply tools in the search for better understanding. Finally, it must be emphasized that in addition to their use in quality assessment, statistics must become an integral part of the objective decision making during peer review.

Suggested Readings

Bailar, J. C., and Mosteller, F., editors. *Medical Uses of Statistics.* Boston: Massachusetts Medical Society, 1986.

Cohn, V. *News and Numbers.* Ames, IA: Iowa State University Press, 1989.

Colton, T. *Statistics in Medicine.* Boston: Little, Brown and Co., 1974.

Feinstein, A. R. Scientific standards and epidemiological studies of the menace of daily life. *Science* 24(2):1257–63, Dec. 1988.

Chapter Four

Mortality and Other Outcome Data

Jennifer Daley, M.D.

Measurement of the effectiveness of medical care in hospital quality assurance has been dominated by investigations into the process of providing the technical aspects of care. Such process evaluation measures what health care providers do to and for patients and, conversely, how patients seek medical care and respond to recommended plans or therapies.[1] The impact of this process on patients' health status is called *outcome*. Medical "outcomes are those changes, either favorable or adverse, in the actual or potential health status of persons, groups, or communities that can be attributed to prior or concurrent care."[2] Broadly defined, patient health status includes the physical, psychological, social, and attitudinal aspects of patients' lives. Although much effort has been expended on developing criteria, norms, and standards for the process evaluation of technical care, relatively little emphasis has been placed on developing measurement techniques to assess outcome.[3-8]

The relationship between the technical process of care and clinical outcome is difficult to determine. Few accepted medical practices have enough solid evidence from well-controlled studies to establish this relationship.[9-11] Because improvements or deteriorations in health status must be adjusted for other intervening factors that contribute to any change in outcome before they can be attributed to medical care, outcome measurement is an indirect means of assessing the effectiveness of medical practice.

Several obstacles prohibit outcome from being used as a direct measurement of effectiveness. Important and relevant outcomes may occur at some time removed from the medical care given, and information may be difficult to collect, may be inaccurate, or may reflect other interventions that cannot be assessed.[12] Although some outcome measures can be collected concurrently during hospitalization (for example, in-hospital mortality or the incidence of decubitus ulcers among patients), indicators of patient outcome generally must be collected after hospitalization has ended. As a result, accurate information about outcomes that occur after hospitalization or outpatient visits has not generally been measured in quality assurance programs.

Using health status outcomes as sole measures of the effectiveness of an intervention also assumes that all the other factors that can influence the outcome have been adjusted for. Confounding factors include other diagnoses, procedures, patient attributes, and environmental characteristics, and the contribution of each of these factors to different outcomes must be measured. Even after adjustments for diagnosis, procedure, patient characteristics, and psychosocial and environmental factors have been made, attributing significant changes in outcome to the medical care without actually reviewing the process of care is difficult.[13]

However, despite these limitations, the measurement of outcome in assessing medical care has increasingly become the focus of hospital quality assurance. Screening for adverse outcomes such as nosocomial infections, in-hospital mortality in patients admitted for minor surgery, and maternal mortality has been utilized in hospital quality assurance for many years.[14-16] The occurrence of these adverse outcomes has been used to target audit activity and improve the yield of QA resources. Increased scrutiny of the outcome of medical interventions has accompanied efforts to control the inflationary costs of medical care in the past decade. Much of this new focus has emanated from the efforts of regulatory agencies and health services researchers to evaluate the impact of medical care on patient health status in an era of cost containment and to search for treatments that are cost-effective.[17] More attention to the positive and adverse outcomes attributable to medical care has been demanded by regulatory agencies, the business community, and consumer groups seeking accountability from the medical profession and hospital management.[18]

Although outcome research has been an area of academic investigation for several years,[19-21] the public release of comparative hospital mortality rates by the Health Care Financing Administration (HCFA) in 1987 and subsequent years brought unprecedented attention to hospital and mortality data and other medical outcomes.[22-24] Committed to the release of comparative mortality data to the public, HCFA has also undertaken the analysis of its extensive data bases with the goal of assessing the cost and effectiveness of medical interventions in the Medicare population.[25,26] Concurrently, the Joint Commission on Accreditation of Healthcare Organizations (Joint Commission) announced the Agenda for Change, its broad initiative to refocus hospital quality assurance on the outcomes of medical care.[27] In health services research, the analysis of variations in practice patterns and the outcome of medical and surgical practice in both hospital-based and ambulatory care are actively being investigated.[28-34]

All these initiatives make understanding the strengths and limitations of the use of outcome assessment in hospital quality assurance imperative. This chapter discusses outcome assessment from several vantage points. First, it describes the types of outcome measures commonly available for use in hospital QA programs. Second, it reviews hospital mortality data and the history of their use in assessing the effectiveness of medical care in hospitals. The chapter then outlines the conceptual issues that should be considered in assessing the use of outcome data in hospital quality assurance and employs these criteria to explore, in detail, the strengths and limitations of using hospital mortality data in hospital quality assurance. HCFA's comparative mortality data are used in a detailed example. Finally, the chapter briefly discusses the use of outcome data other than mortality data in hospital quality assurance.

☐ Outcome Measures in Hospital Quality Assurance

Outcome measures advocated for use in assessing the effectiveness of care in hospital quality assurance include hospital-associated mortality rates,[35-41] rates of readmission to the hospital for continued therapy in the same episode of illness,[42-44] nosocomial infections,[45-48] complications associated with hospitalization,[49-51] disability,[52] positive or adverse changes in physiologic status,[53] and patient satisfaction with health care.[54-56] Table 4-1 displays technical and interpersonal categories of outcome measures and includes specific examples of measures available in hospital quality assurance in each category.

Table 4-1. Categories of Outcome Measures

Category	Examples
Technical care:	
Mortality for specific diseases, conditions, procedures, and populations	• Infant mortality • Maternal mortality • Age- and sex-adjusted mortality
Preventable mortality, morbidity, and disability	• Sentinel events (for example, in-hospital death after low-risk procedure)
Disease- or condition-specific measurements of physiologic outcomes	• Blood pressure in hypertensives under treatment • Blood sugar in diabetics treated with insulin, diet, and/or hypoglycemic therapy
Presence of conditions that represent treatment failures	• Decubitus ulcers developed during hospital stay • Hospital readmission for complications or inadequate therapy on previous admission
Complications during or following therapy	• Nosocomial infections • Postoperative complications
Changes in functional status	• Physical changes • Mental changes • Psychosocial changes
Interpersonal care:	
Patient dissatisfaction with care	• Access • Convenience • Financial assistance
Maladaptation to chronic illness	• Pain control • Sense of well-being • Energy level

Hospital Mortality Data: From Past to Present

Preventing avoidable deaths and prolonging life in the face of illness and injury are primary goals of modern medical care. In the 19th century, Farr and other British epidemiologists urged physicians to publish local mortality statistics as a measure of a community's health.[57] In the 20th century, the publication of disease-specific rates of illness and mortality for common illnesses has become a routine means of assessing the public health.[58] Vital statistics are kept as a crude but valuable index of the health of the general population.[59] However, the use of population-based mortality statistics is not appropriate in assessing the effectiveness of hospital care.

Florence Nightingale first suggested the use of hospital-specific mortality rates to measure the effectiveness of care rendered in hospitals.[60] Appalled by the high mortality rates among soldiers admitted to field hospitals in Crimea, she argued that the routine observation of variation among hospital mortality rates would supply good evidence regarding the quality of the care rendered in the hospitals. Observing considerable variation in hospital mortality rates between the British general hospitals (7.9 percent) and the workhouses and special hospitals that cared for the poor (11.5 percent), she conceded that she was unable to attribute the differences in mortality rates to the care rendered in the hospitals or to the burden of illness in patients admitted to different hospitals.[61]

Early in the 20th century, E. A. Codman, a surgeon at Massachusetts General Hospital in Boston, argued that hospitals should monitor the end results of care rendered. One of the earliest proponents of outcome-based evaluation, he asserted that if treatment did not achieve the intended outcome, preventable or avoidable causes should be sought and modified in the future for other patients. In terms of mortality, Codman recognized that there were two kinds: one occurring by chance and hence unavoidable and the other "intentional" and dependent on both the risk of the patient's death prior to treatment and the skill of the surgeon.[62] Classic epidemiologic studies of maternal mortality in New York City in the early 1930s revealed an alarmingly high rate of maternal and infant mortality.[63] Sixty-four percent of all maternal deaths were preventable, and almost half of these preventable deaths were attributed to errors in judgment or technique by the attending physician or midwife.

Variation in hospital mortality rates came to the attention of health care epidemiologists again in the 1960s. An unanticipated finding of the National Halothane Study, designed to determine whether the anesthetic was responsible for hepatic necrosis, was a 24-fold difference in the crude surgical fatality rates among the 34 university teaching hospitals voluntarily participating in the study.[64,65] After adjustment for age, physical status, operation type, and the likelihood of shock, the differences were reduced by about threefold; however, significant unexplained variation in the adjusted mortality rates among institutions persisted. More sophisticated case-mix adjustment and evaluation of the impact of not operating on patients with similar clinical conditions were required to determine the contribution of case mix to the variation in surgical mortality rates. Subsequent studies of variation in mortality rates demonstrated that adjustment for a limited number of patient characteristics reduces variation in mortality.[66,67] Some surgical procedures still had significant variation in mortality, which the study attributed to effectiveness of care, but these findings were not validated with chart review.

The relationship between hospital mortality and the volume of patients cared for in selected surgical procedures has been investigated in several studies.[68-79] Analysis of a large sample of hospital discharge abstracts from the Commission on Professional and Hospital Activities (CPHA) for 12 selected surgical conditions revealed that lower mortality rates occur in hospitals performing more operations each year in open-heart surgery, transurethral resection of the prostate, and vascular surgery but not in cholecystectomy and total hip replacement.[80] Investigation of a large national data base of medical and surgical cases concluded that in surgical cases the volume of surgery performed in a hospital inversely correlates with hospital mortality, but a similar relationship among medical patients was not observed.[81,82] A more recent analysis of six surgical conditions in more than 500 hospitals noted a nonlinear relationship between surgical volume and mortality with minimum mortality at volumes of surgery higher than those of the average-size hospital.[83]

Pursuing the hypothesis that variations in hospital mortality rates reflect differences in the effectiveness of care among hospitals, others have investigated the relationship of hospital structure and mortality. Roemer and Friedman studied a large number of hospitals in the 1960s and noted that higher degrees of medical staff organization were correlated with lower hospital mortality rates.[84] Shortell and LoGerfo reported on the in-hospital mortality rate for 50,000 acute myocardial infarctions in one region of the country and noted that medical staff organization and physician participation in policy and decision making had a positive correlation with better outcome.[85] Flood and others studied surgical morbidity and mortality in a national sampling of surgical patients and concluded that surgical staff coordination and specialty differentiation were strongly associated with good outcomes.[86]

One early study used mortality data in selected disease-specific categories to assess the quality of care in English teaching and nonteaching hospitals and demonstrated a wide range of unadjusted case fatality rates in selected disease categories.[87] After adjustments for age and sex, the case fatality rates were closer, but significant variation persisted that could be attributed either to better medical care in the teaching hospitals or to differences in the patients admitted to the teaching and nonteaching hospitals.

HCFA Mortality Data: An Overview

Although research and academic interest have focused on hospital mortality data for several decades, the 1986 release through the Freedom of Information Act of a crude analysis of 1984 hospital mortality rates by HCFA drew unprecedented attention to the appropriate analysis and interpretation of hospital mortality rates. The 1986 mortality data analysis had several significant methodological limitations,[88,89] including limited adjustment for diagnoses, comorbidities, and the use of in-hospital mortality as the outcome measure. Committed to continuing the release of hospital mortality data, HCFA has extended and revised the mortality analysis in each subsequent year (1987, 1988, 1989). Figure 4-1 summarizes some of the features of the HCFA comparative mortality data releases.

The data base that HCFA employs in calculating the annual hospital mortality rates includes patient characteristics and demographic information from the MedPAR data base. The MedPAR file includes all the information submitted by hospitals to fiscal intermediaries and HCFA for reimbursement under prospective payment. The MedPAR file includes all the information outlined in figure 4-2.

This information is merged with Social Security death benefit data to determine the survival status of each beneficiary admitted to an acute care hospital during the calendar year under analysis. In the mortality analysis, HCFA includes only the last discharge of the calendar year for each beneficiary from an acute care hospital. For example, a patient admitted three times during 1987 to two different hospitals has only the last admission included in the analysis, and that patient is included in the cases attributed to the last hospital from which he or she was discharged.

In the analysis of the mortality data, HCFA divides all the cases in the file into 16 diagnostic categories based on the principal diagnosis. Ten of the diagnostic categories are associated with a high risk of death: severe acute heart disease, severe chronic heart disease, chronic pulmonary disease, chronic renal disease, severe trauma, infectious diseases (sepsis), stroke, cancer, gastrointestinal catastrophes, and metabolic and electrolyte disturbances. Diagnostic categories with a low risk of death are gynecologic disease, urologic disease, orthopedic conditions, low-risk heart disease, gastrointestinal disease, and ophthalmologic disease. Principal diagnoses not falling into one of these categories are included in an "all other cases" category.

Figure 4-1. Health Care Financing Administration (HCFA) Comparative Hospital Mortality Data

Data Base
- Includes all Medicare discharges from acute care hospitals
- Covers calendar years 1986, 1987, 1988
- Includes only the last hospital discharge of each Medicare beneficiary during the calendar year
- Uses MedPAR data for clinical and demographic information
- Uses Social Security death benefit information to determine survival status

Analysis
- Establishes 16 diagnostic categories (10 high-risk and 6 low-risk for death) based on the principal diagnosis
- Sets outcome measure at survival status at 30 days after admission
- Uses logistic regression to adjust for clinical risk adjustment
- Makes adjustments for:
  - Patient age
  - Transfer status
  - Admission source
  - Prior hospitalizations
  - Limited comorbidities based on secondary diagnoses

Report Format
- Includes all years of data since 1986
- Determines within each year, for each of the 16 diagnostic categories and for all discharges:
  - The total number of cases discharged
  - The actual 30-day mortality rate for those cases
  - The range of predicted mortality rates from the analytic model

Figure 4-2. Variables Available in Secondary Data Bases

- Age
- Sex
- Principal diagnosis for which the patient was admitted and up to five secondary diagnoses
- Principal procedure and up to three secondary procedures
- Type of admission (emergency, urgent, elective, newborn)
- Discharge status (alive or dead); if discharged alive, the place discharged to (for example, home, skilled nursing facility)
- Transfer status if the patient was transferred from another acute care hospital within the same day
- Date of admission
- Date of discharge

The HCFA analysis adjusts for several patient characteristics that can independently influence hospital-associated mortality: patient age, patient sex, the number of hospitalizations in the six months prior to the last discharge of the calendar year, comorbid conditions, transfer status, admission source (for example, home, nursing home), and admission type (for example, emergency, elective). The comorbid conditions adjusted for in the analysis are limited to the presence of secondary diagnoses of cancer, chronic cardiovascular disease, and chronic liver disease in the 1988 mortality data release.

The outcome measure used in HCFA's mortality analyses is 30-day postadmission mortality rather than in-hospital mortality. Thirty-day mortality differs from in-hospital mortality in two ways. Thirty-day mortality includes patients who died within 30 days of admission even if they have been discharged from the hospital and excludes patients who died in the hospital but whose death occurred more than 30 days after admission.

Using a statistical technique called *logistic regression,* HCFA's mortality analysis attempts to adjust hospital mortality rates for differences in the types of patients each hospital admits each year. Using information from the more than six million Medicare beneficiaries admitted to hospitals each year, a predictive model is constructed that estimates the contribution of the patients' clinical characteristics to the risk of dying within 30 days of admission. Using this model and the relative weighting of the patient characteristics, the model is then used to calculate an estimated probability of each patient dying within 30 days of admission if the patient with identical characteristics was taken care of in a typical hospital. Once the predicted probability of death has been estimated for each patient, the mortality rates for each hospital are calculated by a process of averaging. The hospital's "predicted mortality rate" is the average of the estimated probability of death for each patient whose last admission during the year was to the hospital.

The HCFA mortality report for each hospital includes data calculated for each of the years for which data are available using the most current HCFA methodology. For example, the 1988 data release includes mortality data calculated using the 1988 methodology for 1986, 1987, and 1988. For each year and each diagnostic category and all cases, HCFA reports three figures: the number of cases, the actual mortality rate, and the range of predicted mortality rates. The number of cases includes all Medicare beneficiaries, both those who lived and those who died, whose last discharge was from that hospital during the calendar year under study. The actual hospital mortality rates are obtained by dividing the number of patients who died within 30 days of admission by the total number of cases in the diagnostic category and are expressed as a percentage.

The presentation of a predicted range of mortality rates reflects statistical uncertainty in the model. Three sources of uncertainty are present in the models HCFA uses to calculate the predicted mortality. The first source of uncertainty is random chance. Death is an infrequent event, and variation from year to year in a hospital's overall mortality rate and within each diagnostic category is expected. Smaller hospitals and hospitals with only a few cases in each diagnostic category will have more random variation. As hospital size and the number of cases in each diagnostic category increase, the random variation in hospital-associated mortality is reduced. As a result of random variation, the predicted ranges for small hospitals, diagnostic categories with small numbers of patients, and diagnostic categories in which death is a rare event (for example, the low-risk diagnostic categories) will be wide. Large hospitals and hospitals that admit a large number of patients in high- or low-risk categories will notice that the prediction interval or range is narrower. To quantify the amount of random variation in hospital mortality rates, HCFA uses the 95th percent confidence interval limit. The 95th percent confidence interval is a statistical statement of the random variation in hospital mortality rates, but it makes no statement about the clinical confidence in the estimated mortality rates. The other sources of uncertainty in the model are risk factors associated with mortality that are not included in the model and variation in the effectiveness of the care provided by the hospitals.

☐ Criteria for Evaluating Outcome Measures in Quality Assurance

Figure 4-3 outlines 10 criteria that should be used in evaluating outcome measures in quality assurance. The following discussion applies those criteria to HCFA hospital mortality data as an example of a widely available measure of outcome.

Criterion 1: Clinical Relevance of the Measure in Assessing the Effectiveness of the Care Provided by the Hospital

For example, what potentially preventable problems are targeted for review? The goal of reviewing mortality associated with hospitalization is the identification of deaths that occurred in circumstances that can be prevented or avoided in the future. Some deaths always indicate circumstances that should be investigated for preventable problems in the effectiveness of care. In 1976, Rutstein and others proposed a negative scale to monitor the outcome of poor quality of care; they identified the occurrence of unnecessary disease or disability or unnecessary, untimely deaths as warning signals or

Figure 4-3. Criteria for Evaluating Outcome Data in Quality Assurance

1. *Clinical relevance of the measure in assessing the effectiveness of the care provided by the hospital.* For example, what potentially preventable problems are targeted for review?
2. *Source of the outcome data.* Can the outcome measure be collected during the patient's hospitalization? If so, what will be required to collect the data concurrently during hospitalization? If not, what are the sources of posthospitalization information (for example, the patient, the patient's family, the attending physician, insurance claims data)?
3. *Reliability of the outcome measure.* How can the reliability of the outcome measure be determined? What factors need to be considered?
4. *Appropriate measurement of outcome.* When does observation for outcome begin? How long after a procedure, hospitalization, or visit should outcome be measured? If the measure is collected after discharge, what are the intervening variables that could confound the outcome measure?
5. *Frequency of outcome occurrence.* If the outcome measure occurs rarely, how many occurrences are needed in order for the outcome measure to be statistically meaningful?
6. *Dependence of outcome on the patient's diagnosis or procedure.* What means are available to adjust for the case mix of the patients?
7. *Adjustment for risk factors that influence outcome.* What clinical characteristics of the patient need to be collected? What statistical methods are used to adjust outcome for risk factors?
8. *Effect on the analysis of patient preference regarding outcome.* Are methods available to adjust for the patient's preference regarding outcome?
9. *Validity of outcome measure in assessing effectiveness of medical care.* Can comparison of the rates of outcomes among hospitals be used to evaluate effectiveness of care? Are the differences among hospitals related to differences in the patients admitted to the hospitals or to the effectiveness of the care provided?
10. *Correlation of one outcome measure with other such measures.* For example, how do readmission rates correlate with hospital mortality rates? If there is a good correlation among outcome measurements, what does that imply about effectiveness of care? What are appropriate ways to verify and validate these findings?

sentinel events, indicating that the quality of care could be improved.[90] Examples of sentinel events include maternal death and in-hospital deaths after elective surgery for conditions with which death is rarely associated. In most QA programs, these unexpected deaths are flagged for review on a case-by-case basis. Deaths among patients admitted to the hospital for low-risk elective surgery (for example, tonsillectomy, inguinal hernia repair, and dilatation and curettage) should prompt review of the care delivered.

A case-by-case review of individual deaths is a routine part of hospital QA programs. One mechanism for case review in teaching hospitals has been a departmental morbidity and mortality conference in which peers review the care rendered to patients who died in the preceding month or quarter. Alternatively, members of the QA committee review all the deaths in a specific department, service, or area of the hospital (for example, recovery room, operating room, special care unit, or emergency room). Patients whose deaths were unanticipated and those who died within some period of time after a major intervention (for example, surgery or diagnostic procedure) or after a transfer from one level of intensity of care to another (for example, unanticipated returns to the intensive care unit) may be targeted for in-depth review.

Another traditional source from which potentially avoidable deaths are identified is through the retrospective review of autopsy data. The clinical pathological conference and tissue committee reviews are intended to identify the extent to which the appropriate diagnosis, treatment, and management of complications can be confirmed by postmortem examination. Autopsy review occasionally reveals a complication that might have been avoided or a diagnosis that was unsuspected and should have been entertained and managed prior to the patient's death.[91]

Few studies have assessed the incidence of preventable deaths in medical and surgical patients. Most of these studies have been done to determine the incidence and variation in maternal mortality rates.[92] Remarkably few medical conditions have been studied for preventable deaths. One study in England and another in New Zealand focused on patients who died during treatment of acute asthma. Compared with a group of similar asthma patients who did not die, 46 percent of the patients who died had evidence of preventable complications resulting from treatment.[93,94]

Criterion 2: Source of the Outcome Data

Can the outcome measure be collected during the patient's hospitalization? If so, what will be required to collect the data? If not, what are the sources of posthospitalization information (for example, the patient, the patient's family, the attending physician, and insurance claims data)?

Mortality data that include in-hospital deaths are available in many hospital information systems. Comparative data bases that may also include some information about mortality status within a short period of time after discharge are called secondary data bases because they were developed for a purpose other than mortality or other clinical assessment, usually as a means for reimbursement. Collected by Medicare, other payers, and state health data commissions, these data have been investigated in an effort to demonstrate and explain utilization patterns and are now being used to study the effectiveness of medical care. These comparative data bases include information about patients' demographic characteristics and a brief abstract of the patients' diagnoses and procedures. When hospitals submit bills for services rendered to third-party payers, an abstract of the patient's clinical condition accompanies the financial information. This discharge abstract is defined in different ways by different payers. The Medicare discharge abstract (UB 82) includes the information shown in figure 4-2.

The only currently available source of comparative mortality data for many hospitals is that provided by HCFA. These data indicate comparative hospital mortality rates for acute care hospitals and include only information about Medicare beneficiaries. Many state hospital associations are developing comparative mortality data bases and will make these data available to member hospitals.

Criterion 3: Reliability of the Outcome Measure

Several factors determine the reliability of the information in secondary data bases. Errors in the assignment of the principal diagnosis and procedure are common. Prior to the use of diagnosis-related groups (DRGs) for case-based reimbursement, the Institute of Medicine studied the reliability of abstracted data by comparing medical record face sheets with reabstracted records. Although some data elements were abstracted with good reliability (for example, age and gender), the procedures and diagnoses were unreliably abstracted.[95,96] Since the implementation of the prospective payment system (PPS), the Inspector General has abstracted a nationally representative sample of 7,050 medical records from October 1984 to March 1985 and has found discrepancies in DRG assignment in 20 percent of the cases.[97] Dubois and others studied more than 200,000 medical and surgical admissions to 93 hospitals in an investor-owned chain. Review of a subsample of these admissions in selected diagnoses noted a similar 20 percent rate of disagreement in the principal diagnosis, but the coding errors were equally distributed among hospitals with high and low mortality rates.[98]

Incomplete coding of secondary diagnoses and procedures may vary from hospital to hospital. Jencks and others studied the correlation of coding secondary diagnoses for chronic illness (for example, hypertension, diabetes mellitus, obesity, benign prostatic hypertrophy, and osteoarthritis) with mortality in Medicare patients admitted with stroke, pneumonia, myocardial infarction, and congestive heart failure. Patients with any of these secondary diagnoses had a reduced risk of death, suggesting that chronic diseases are undercoded as secondary diagnoses in patients with life-threatening illnesses.[99] Differences also exist in hospital policies with regard to the coding of admission, discharge, and transfer status. Finally, death, a critical part of any mortality analysis, may not be reliably recorded.[100] Although the quality of information has been suspect in the past, the accuracy of the discharge abstract data has been improving in response to PPS which assigns a DRG based on the clinical data abstract and calculates payment on the basis of the DRG.

Criterion 4: Appropriate Measurement of Outcome

When does observation for outcome begin? How long after a procedure, hospitalization, or visit should outcome be measured? If the measure is collected after discharge, what are the intervening variables that could confound the outcome measure?

Controversy surrounds the appropriate measurement of patient survival status. Different points have been used to begin observation of the patient in determining hospital-associated mortality; some studies measure the time from admission, the time from surgery or major procedure, or the time from discharge to the day of death. Variation also exists in the total observation period, and agreement about whether to use in-hospital mortality or some fixed period of time after admission, discharge, or surgical procedure has been a problem. Using in-hospital mortality is confounded by length of stay, which is heavily dependent on geographic differences in patterns of discharge planning, the availability of nursing homes and other alternative care sites, and hospital policy.[101] Nevertheless, most studies use in-hospital mortality because they lack the capacity to accurately measure patients who died after discharge from the hospital.

As mentioned previously, HCFA mortality data identify deaths within 30 days from the day of admission to the hospital. Thirty-day mortality includes discharged patients who died either at home or another postdischarge facility such as a nursing home and excludes patients who died in the hospital after a stay of longer than 30 days. Deaths occurring after hospitalization but within 30 days of admission that are unrelated to care received in the hospital may be inappropriately attributed to the hospital from which the patient was discharged.

Criterion 5: Frequency of Outcome Occurrence

If the outcome measure occurs rarely, how many occurrences are needed in order for the outcome measure to be statistically meaningful? Despite the fact that nearly one-half of all deaths that occur annually in the United States take place in hospitals, death is the outcome of only 3 percent of all hospital admissions.[102] As a result, a considerable amount of variation in hospital-associated mortality rates exists because of random chance.[103] Some of this random variation can be reduced by reviewing several years of data and combining related procedures and diseases, although the correlation among several medical diseases with high mortality rates[104] or surgical procedures[105] is weak. Relatively little research has been devoted to the effect of small sample sizes in infrequently occurring outcomes such as hospital-associated mortality, and the validity of aggregating mortality or other infrequent outcomes over several years or focusing exclusively on high mortality conditions has not been explored.

Criterion 6: Dependence of Outcome on the Patient's Diagnosis or Procedure

What means are available to adjust for the case-mix of the patients? Hospitals may differ markedly in the range of patients admitted with different diagnoses and procedures. Studies of hospital-associated mortality rates usually attempt to adjust for differences in hospital case mix in one of several ways. Many of the studies limit their analyses to a single disease or procedure.[106,107] Others limit their studies to specialized units in the hospital, for example, neonatal[108] or adult respiratory and surgical intensive care units.[109-111] Others adjust for case mix by using *ICD-9-CM* diagnoses[112] or procedures[113] or use a combination of diagnoses and procedures.[114] Some use DRGs to adjust for case-mix differences across hospitals. Because DRGs are aggregated into homogeneous groups of diagnoses and procedures with regard to length of stay and resource use rather than hospital mortality, DRGs are not a suitable means for case-mix adjustment in mortality studies.[115]

Few well-controlled studies have been conducted to determine the impact of case-mix and risk adjustment on understanding the variation in mortality rates. Hebel and others studied the variation in crude mortality rates among four hospitals in a large metropolitan area.[116] One hospital's crude mortality rate was twice that of the other three. Case-mix adjustment using primary diagnoses reduced the variation in mortality rates considerably. The authors concluded that the variation in mortality rates was due to severity of illness and referral patterns in the community.

Criterion 7: Adjustment for Risk Factors That Influence Outcome

What clinical characteristics of the patient need to be collected? What statistical methods are used to adjust outcome for risk factors?

Adjusting for the patient's risk of death on admission to the hospital has been difficult for most studies attempting to use hospital mortality to draw conclusions about effectiveness of care. Not all patients come into the hospital with the same risk of dying; how sick or near death the patients are on arrival at the hospital must be adjusted for. In addition to the diagnosis or procedure for which patients are admitted, their risk of dying varies with the burden of acute or chronic illness on admission. Methods and measurements to account for variations in patients' risk of death on admission (known as adjustments for severity of illness) exist, but the use of hospital mortality data to evaluate hospital care presents problems. Assessment of the patient's condition *at the time of admission* is critical in order to be able to immediately assess the patient prior to any intervention by medical care personnel. Assessments taken *after admission* may be confounded by the care given to the patient and the patient's response to that care.

Factors that need to be taken into account when assessing the patient's risk of death on admission are outlined in figure 4-4. Possible sources of information about the patient's risk status on admission include secondary data such as the discharge data available from billing information (for example, the use of secondary diagnoses). These data have limitations because it is difficult to know whether the secondary diagnoses were present on admission or occurred later during hospitalization. One study in the Medicare population has identified the presence of secondary diagnoses of chronic disease as inversely correlated with the likelihood of death.[117] The authors offer the hypothesis that critically ill patients may be less likely to have secondary diagnoses for chronic illness coded. Conversely, a study of nearly 3,000 cancer patients from seven hospitals in California noted that adjustment for coexisting comorbid conditions accounted for most of the variation in mortality rates among the hospitals.[118]

Other information about the patient's risk of death on admission is available by reviewing the chart for measures of the factors mentioned previously. Attempts to standardize and measure these factors have been actively investigated in recent years. Several scoring and measurement systems have been developed for categorizing patients into similar groups of case mix and severity.[119] Two of the systems—Computerized Disease Staging[120] and Patient Management Categories[121]—rely on discharge abstract data to assign a severity score. The other three systems—APACHE II,[122] MEDISGRPS,[123] and the Computerized Severity Index (CSI)[124]—require chart review to obtain the necessary information to calculate a severity score or the likelihood of death.

Knaus and others studied the variation in mortality rates among patients admitted to adult respiratory and surgical intensive care units.[125] Using the APACHE score, which includes patient age, indication for admission, a comorbidity score, and a 12-item score for the patient's physiologic condition on admission, analysis revealed that most of the variation in hospital mortality rates could be accounted for by differences in the severity of illness. Pollack and others used the Physiologic Stability Index (PSI), a measure of patients' risk of dying, to study the variation in in-hospital mortality rates among patients admitted to pediatric intensive care units. Noting considerable variation among nine units, the study demonstrated that the variation in mortality rates in pediatric intensive care units is accounted for by adjustment for severity of illness.[126] Dubois and others studied the impact of severity-of-illness measures on the variation in hospital mortality rates among a group of hospitals in which the actual mortality rates were lower than predicted (the low outliers) and a group of hospitals in which the actual death rates were higher than predicted (the high outliers).[127,128] Using the APACHE score and a few other variables to adjust for severity on admission in three medical conditions (stroke, pneumonia, and myocardial infarction), most of the two-fold variation between the high- and low-outlier hospitals was explained by the severity adjustment. However, about 10 percent of the variation remained unexplained.

In response to criticism of HCFA's release of hospital-specific mortality rates,[129,130] HCFA developed a microcomputer-based system, the Medicare Mortality Predictor System (MMPS), to produce predicted mortality rates adjusted for clinical condition on admission in four medical conditions (stroke, congestive heart failure, pneumonia, and acute myocardial infarction) that represent about one-eighth of all Medicare admissions

Figure 4-4. Patient Characteristics That Contribute to Risk of Death

- Physiologic status on admission (for example, presence or absence of fever, shock, respiratory distress, coma).
- Burden of chronic illness (for example, presence or absence of comorbid conditions such as cancer, renal failure, chronic cardiac or respiratory failure).
- Functional status (for example, ability to be independent in activities of daily living, degree of dependency on others).
- Patient's preference about the goals of his or her medical care. In adjusting for patient preference in mortality data, adjustment must be made for directives about cardiopulmonary resuscitation and requests for supportive or palliative care (for example, do-not-resuscitate orders, "care and comfort measures only," durable power of attorney for health care).

and one-third of Medicare mortality.[131] Using a limited number of clinical variables measured within the first 24 hours of admission, the MMPS predictors accounted for approximately one-sixth to one-quarter of the variability in mortality among individual patients. The remaining variation may have been accounted for by random variability among patients, risk factors not measured by the risk model, or effectiveness of care.

Evaluation of the variation in mortality rates at the hospital level among Medicare patients in the four MMPS conditions revealed that the majority of the variation in annual mortality rates was chance variability due to the small numbers of patients admitted each year to most hospitals. Using the MMPS data, the addition of clinical risk adjustment reduced the variability between observed and unadjusted mortality national rates by about one-third.[132]

In general, three statistical methods are used to adjust mortality data for differences in case mix and patient characteristics: linear regression, indirect standardization, and logistic regression. All three techniques use a schedule of mortality rates for each level of the clinical characteristics and calculate an expected mortality rate that can be compared with the observed mortality rate. Having adjusted for these risk factors in the model, differences between observed and expected mortality rates cannot be attributed to the patient characteristics in the model. Each technique differs in the way in which the schedule of mortality rates is calculated and how the differences between observed and predicted mortality rates are calculated.

Logistic regression is used in many mortality analyses because the dependent variable is dichotomous (dead or alive) and the probability of the outcome event (death) is small. However, use of the technique does assume that the relationship between the predictors and the natural logarithm of the odds of dying is linear. Logistic regression generates equations in which the regression coefficients represent average values within each of the independent variables. An individual's probability of death (a number between zero and one) is calculated by substituting his or her values for the clinical characteristics in the equation and multiplying by the regression coefficients.

Criterion 8: Effect on the Analysis of Patient Preference Regarding Outcome

Are methods available to adjust for the patient's preference regarding outcome? A critical element of every outcome assessment is the value that the patient places on his or her own health status. The patient's preference with regard to outcome has been an element of outcome assessment that has been largely ignored. In general, with respect to hospital-associated mortality, death is held to be an undesirable outcome. Increasingly, however, among some patients with advanced malignancy, end-stage cardiac or neurologic disease, or irreversible organ failure, comfort measures and a painless and comfortable death are what is sought from the palliative services of the hospital. Care must be taken in any mortality analysis to account for the patient's preferences with regard to death. Note should be taken of the patient's or the patient's family's wishes with respect to do-not-resuscitate orders. Accounting for the patient's goals in seeking medical care is even more significant in adjusting outcomes related to improvements in functional status and psychological adjustment.

Criterion 9: Validity of Outcome Measure in Assessing Effectiveness of Medical Care

Can comparison of the rates of outcomes among hospitals be used to evaluate effectiveness of care? Are the differences among hospitals related to the differences in the patients admitted to the hospitals or the effectiveness of the care provided?

Several limitations of using comparative mortality data to assess effectiveness of hospital care have been reviewed. Collected for other purposes, the data may be inaccurate and therefore misleading. Random chance plays a significant part in the variation in hospital mortality rates from year to year because death is a relatively rare event. Even in the most common conditions in the Medicare population, chance variation accounts for the majority of differences in mortality rates. Care must be used in interpreting comparative in-hospital mortality rates because of the potential bias in different hospital discharge policies. Use of 30-day postadmission mortality eliminates the length-of-stay bias but may result in hospitals having deaths attributed to them, when, in fact, the patient died of some unrelated event. Assessment of the value the patient places on life and death and, consequently, the outcome of medical care must be incorporated to adjust for the patient's preference with regard to outcome. Finally, the patient's risk of dying on arrival at the hospital and prior to the initiation of care must be adjusted for in order to appropriately group patients with similar levels of risk.

Given all these factors, effectiveness of care clearly cannot be judged from reviewing comparative hospital mortality data alone. Hospitals with mortality rates that are higher than most hospitals or a peer group of hospitals may have reason to be concerned about the effectiveness of the care rendered. But only a review of the actual process of care can validate or refute the contention that the hospital's effectiveness falls outside accepted standards.

A few limited studies have investigated the relationship between hospitals with high or low mortality rates and the effectiveness of the care provided. Knaus and others prospectively studied the outcome of over 5,000 patients admitted to intensive care units in 13 tertiary medical centers. One hospital had significantly better mortality results than predicted, while another hospital had 58 percent more deaths than predicted. Hospitals with better-than-predicted mortality rates had a high level of communication and coordination in the intensive care team as opposed to the higher-than-predicted hospitals. The authors concluded that coordination among members of an intensive care unit team has a direct impact on outcome.[133]

Dubois and colleagues investigated the relationship among hospitals that were high and low outliers in a claims analysis of mortality.[134] After adjusting for the patients' risk of dying on admission, explicit and implicit chart review was performed in three high-mortality conditions: pneumonia, stroke, and acute myocardial infarction. Explicit review resulted in no apparent differences in effectiveness of care. After adjustment for differences in patient risk, implicit review demonstrated that patients with stroke and pneumonia had a 5 percent incidence of preventable deaths in high-mortality outlier hospitals as compared to 1 percent preventable deaths in low-mortality outlier hospitals.[135,136] The authors concluded that high-mortality outlier hospitals may have both sicker patients and less effective care.

Hannan and others[137] piloted the use of screening hospital discharge abstract data to target mortality cases for peer review. In their pilot study of mostly surgical cases, they used primary surgical procedures with mortality rates of less than 0.5 percent and death occurring in 24 and 48 hours after surgery, as well as other cardinal secondary diagnoses (infection or wound disruption, renal failure, fluid and electrolyte disturbances, and cardiopulmonary arrest as secondary diagnoses in surgical patients), to identify cases for review. Cases identified for review by these screens had a higher likelihood of having care that departed from professionally recognized standards and that caused or contributed to patient death.

The Veterans Administration (VA) conducted a review of hospital mortality rates as a screen for quality of care in 1986.[138] The care of 5.1 percent of the 1,771 deaths in VA medical centers with significantly elevated mortality rates was noted to be definitely or probably not consistent with current medical practice. The study identified apparent differences in mortality among patients admitted to the medical and surgical wards of primarily psychiatric medical centers. In medical and surgical facilities, 3.7 percent of 1,045 deaths were determined to have quality-of-care problems.

Criterion 10: Correlation of One Outcome Measure with Other Such Measures

For example, how do readmission rates correlate with hospital mortality rates? If there is a good correlation among outcome measurements, what does that imply about effectiveness of care? What are appropriate ways to verify and validate these findings?

Several other outcome measures have been proposed for measuring the effectiveness of hospital care; some of them are discussed in more detail in the next part of this chapter. Hospital mortality is such a rare event that comparative mortality analysis is only appropriate in conditions with sufficiently large numbers of deaths to provide the analysis with statistical power to detect differences. Presumably, other outcome measures short of hospital-associated mortality would measure changes in health status that are less severe or extreme. Virtually no research exists that correlates the findings of comparative mortality analyses and other outcome measures, and no studies have directly compared hospitals or hospital outliers in mortality and other outcome measures. Further research will be required to establish correlations among outcomes and to validate their usefulness in assessing the effectiveness of hospital care.

☐ Outcome Measures Other Than Mortality

Much of the focus on potentially preventable events during hospitalization has been on the concurrent detection of events that, in general, signal a poor outcome resulting from a process of care that does not meet minimal standards. This method is an extension of the sentinel events described by Rutstein and others, which are used as conditions or episodes that by their very occurrence suggest that the effectiveness of care is suspect.[139] They described three different categories of sentinel events: unnecessary diseases (for example, diphtheria, tetanus, and smallpox), unnecessary disabilities (for example, paralysis from poliomyelitis and birth defects from rubella), and untimely deaths (maternal mortality and death after low-risk surgery such as appendectomy).

Operational adverse occurrence screening for hospital quality assurance was developed during the California Medical Insurance Feasibility Study in which review of 20,000 patients' medical records yielded 20 different in-hospital events that potentially could result in medical malpractice litigation.[140] These in-hospital events have been incorporated into a modified version of potentially adverse outcome occurrence screens that are used in many hospital QA programs.[141] For example, typical adverse occurrence screens include hospital readmissions for complications or further therapy of a condition that had been previously treated during hospitalization, nosocomial infections, unplanned return to an operating room after surgery, admission to an intensive care unit from general floor care, and hospital-related incidents such as falls and injuries.

Most hospitals also have incident reporting systems in which patient accidents and falls, medication errors, and other errors are reported to quality assurance, risk management, and hospital administration. Most of these systems rely on the judgment of the hospital staff, and the extent of reporting depends on the attentiveness and motivation of the staff. The definition of what constitutes a reportable incident varies among institutions, and education programs among nursing staff, medical staff, and other hospital personnel are required to communicate what clinical events should be reported.

Marked variability exists in the definition, identification, and standardization of adverse events. In general, each adverse outcome should trigger further assessment of the care rendered and be used as a means of screening for preventable problems in effectiveness of patient care. Furthermore, some number of false positives are expected, but little data exist to assess the sensitivity and specificity of adverse events as screening tests. In the California Medical Insurance Feasibility Study, 81 percent of the charts that failed the 20 occurrence screens were determined to have no disability caused by medical or patient intervention (the false-positive rate of the screens). Conversely, 5.5 percent of all the records reviewed had evidence of some event that potentially could result in litigation compensation (the true-positive incidence of compensable events).

Some jurisdictions and state and national regulatory agencies require hospitals to report summary statistics on adverse occurrences and incident reports. The Maryland Hospital Association has an ongoing research project to assess the use of a limited number of clinical indicators on which hospitals might be validly compared.[142] Indicators included in the study are nosocomial infections, surgical wound infections, autopsy rates, newborn deaths, perioperative deaths, cesarean sections, hospital readmissions, unplanned admissions following ambulatory surgery, intensive care unit readmissions, and unscheduled returns to the operating room. The Joint Commission has developed clinical indicators to screen for problems in quality of care in several areas: hospital-wide, obstetrics, anesthesia, cardiovascular disease, oncology, and trauma. In addition to developing specific clinical indicators in each area, the Joint Commission collects information on patient risk factors that may influence the occurrence of each potentially adverse outcome. Currently, the most widely used adverse occurrence screening program is the generic quality screens used by HCFA and the Professional Review Organizations (PROs) to monitor the quality of care rendered to hospitalized Medicare beneficiaries.[143]

In conjunction with efforts to reform malpractice legislation in New York, research is currently being conducted by the Harvard Medical Practice Study Group to assess the use of a modified version of the California Medical Insurance Feasibility Study occurrence screens in identifying adverse events and the probability that they could have been averted. The results of this study, which will be available some time in 1990, may shed light on the reliability and validity of using occurrence screens to identify preventable adverse outcomes.

Two specific indicators of potentially adverse outcomes appear in virtually all the screening programs for quality of care: nosocomial infection rates and hospital readmissions. Some of the methodological issues of data collection, analysis, reliability, and validity are briefly discussed for these indicators in the following paragraphs.

Nosocomial Infections

Monitoring the effectiveness of hospital care through the incidence of nosocomial infections has considerable apparent validity because, by definition, nosocomial infections are those acquired in the hospital. Although nosocomial infection rates have been correlated with other measures of outcome of hospitalization, such as prolonged hospitalization,[144] hospital mortality,[145] and hospital readmissions,[146,147] the causal relationship between ineffective or poor care that can be prevented and the acquisition of a hospital-acquired infection has not been definitely established. Indeed, no studies of nosocomial infection rates have been done to compare the effectiveness of care rendered among hospitals.

Nosocomial infections complicate about 6 percent of all acute care hospital admissions.[148] The most common nosocomial infections are urinary tract infections, surgical wound infections, pneumonia, and bacteremia. These four infections account for more than 80 percent of all nosocomial infections, and 70 percent of these infections occur in patients undergoing surgery.[149] The difficulty in reliably determining the presence of a nosocomial infection is one of the greatest limitations to the use of these events as a measure of effectiveness of care. First, it is often difficult to assess whether the patient acquired the infection in the hospital or entered the hospital with the infection. Second, relying on the presence of a written diagnosis of infection in the chart is an inadequate means of screening for infection. Surveillance for nosocomial infection requires the monitoring of laboratory and bacteriology results, X-ray findings, clinical signs and symptoms, and treatment administered, especially antibiotic therapy.[150] Finally, ascertainment of rates of nosocomial infection is very sensitive to the intensity of surveillance in a hospital.[151] Hospitals with intensive monitoring for nosocomial infections report rates of 12 percent to 15 percent in contrast to hospitals with more informal and less intensive surveillance that report rates of 3 percent to 5 percent. In the absence of standardized methods of data collection and disease definition, hospitals with intensive monitoring programs will appear to have higher rates of nosocomial infection than those with less rigorous programs.

Another significant limitation to the use of nosocomial infection rates in assessing hospital quality of care is the critical importance of adjustment for the hospital's case mix and the patients' severity of illness. The risk of acquiring an infection in the hospital is certainly affected by the diagnosis and procedure for which the patient is admitted, as well as by comorbid conditions, medications, physiologic condition on admission, age, sex, hospital service, race, and the urgency of admission.[152,153] Further studies are needed to assess the validity of using comparative nosocomial infection rates to assess hospital quality of care and to determine whether and how such rates correlate with other measures of outcome.

Hospital Readmissions

Reviewing the care of patients who require readmission to the hospital for further therapy or therapy for complications of therapy from a previous hospitalization during the same episode of illness has intuitive appeal in searching for preventable problems in effectiveness of care. Hospital readmission occurs much more frequently than hospital-associated mortality. For example, in the Medicare population about 30 percent of hospitalized beneficiaries are admitted more than once during a single calendar year.[154] Readmissions can occur for many reasons. Patients are readmitted not only because of complications resulting from previous hospitalization, but also for further treatment of recurring chronic conditions such as cancer and congestive heart failure and staged procedures such as cardiac catheterization and coronary artery bypass grafting. Also, some patients who are readmitted may require additional therapy for disease progression or complications unrelated to care provided during the previous admission.

Although the reliability of collecting readmission data seems straightforward, some technical limitations restrict determinations of the incidence and prevalence of hospital readmission. For example, some patients who are readmitted are not readmitted to the same hospital. Thus, analysis of readmission patterns requires a data base that includes all the admissions for the population under study. These data bases generally are insurance claims data bases that are not routinely available to individual hospitals. Additionally, in order to link admissions for individual patients over time, the data base must include some means of identifying the patient uniquely, usually by means of a Social Security number or some variation of the Social Security number. Most insurance claims data bases do not routinely collect this information. Three studies have been conducted using linked claims data to study hospital readmissions. Two studies in the Medicare population used Medicare MedPAR data[155] or CPHA data;[156] the third study used a general population-based Canadian data base.[157]

The definition of the appropriate observation period for readmission related to the care provided during a prior hospitalizatin has received limited attention and requires adjustment for the conditions and patient characteristics under study. Anderson and Steinberg defined such readmission as being within 60 days to any hospital after the day of discharge for the same disease. They sought to determine associated patient characteristics or risk factors that would predict the likelihood of readmission and did not study the validity of studying readmission as a measure of hospital quality of care.[158] Desharnais and others studied the impact of the implementation of PPS on hospital readmission and in-hospital mortality. They defined readmission as an admission to the same hospital within the same quarter of the year and found no impact of PPS after case-mix adjustment for patient characteristics.[159] Roos and others studied readmission for complications for two years after surgery for hysterectomy, cholecystectomy, and prostatectomy as a means of identifying quality-of-care problems and noted promising results in screening for adverse events.[160] None of these studies attempted to investigate the validity of using readmission rates to assess hospital quality of care or their correlation with other measures of outcome.

□ Summary

Many measures of adverse outcomes are available in assessing the outcome of medical care. Each is limited to some extent by the frequency of occurrence of the event, the ease and reliability with which the measure can be collected, and the availability of appropriate methods and data to adjust for differences in case mix and severity of illness. Further research is needed to develop and validate case-mix and severity adjustment methods and to determine the validity of using these measures to identify and correct preventable problems in quality of care that are within the control of hospitals and their staffs. Finally, large-scale studies are needed to determine the significance and correlation of comparative rates of adverse outcomes among hospitals.

References

1. Donabedian, A. *The Definition of Quality and Approaches to Its Management.* Vol. 2, *Explorations in Quality Assessment and Monitoring.* Ann Arbor, MI: Health Administration Press, 1980, p. 81.

2. Donabedian, A. *The Definition of Quality and Approaches to Its Management.* Vol. 3, *The Methods and Findings of Quality Assessment—An Illustrated Analysis.* Ann Arbor, MI: Health Administration Press, 1985, p. 256.

3. Tarlov, A. R., Ware, J. E., Jr., Greenfield S., and others. The Medical Outcomes Study. *Journal of the American Medical Association* 262(7):925–30, Aug. 1989.

4. Reisenberg, D., and Glass, R. M. The Medical Outcomes Study. *Journal of the American Medical Association* 262(7):943, Aug. 1989.

5. Ellwood, P. M. Outcomes management: a technology of experience. *New England Journal of Medicine* 318(23):1549–56, June 1988.

6. Greenfield, S. The state of outcome research: are we on target? *New England Journal of Medicine* 320(17):1142–43, Apr. 1989.

7. Lohr, K. N. Outcome measurement: concepts and questions. *Inquiry* 25(1):37–50, Spring 1987.

8. Luft, H. S., and Hunt, S. S. Evaluating individual hospital quality through outcome statistics. *Journal of the American Medical Association* 255(20):2780–84, May 1986.

9. Berwick, D. M. Health services research and quality of care: assignments for the 1990's. *Medical Care* 27(8):763–71, Aug. 1989.

10. Eddy, D. M. Variations in physician practice: the role of uncertainty. *Health Affairs* 3(2):74–89, Summer 1989.

11. Wennberg, J. E. Dealing with medical practice variations: a proposal for action. *Health Affairs* 3(2):6–32, Summer 1984.

12. Donabedian, A. The quality of care. *Journal of the American Medical Association* 260(12):1743–48, Sept. 1988.

13. Donabedian, The quality of care.

14. Rutstein, D. D., Berenberg, W., Chalmers, T. C., and others. Measuring the quality of medical care. *New England Journal of Medicine* 294(11):582–88, Mar. 1976.

15. Mills, D. H., editor. *Report on the Medical Insurance Feasibility Study.* San Francisco: California Medical Association, 1977.

16. Craddick, J. W. *Medical Management Analysis Series.* Vol. 2, *Improving Quality and Resource Management through Medical Management Analysis.* Rockville, MD: Medical Management Analysis International, Inc., 1987.

17. Roper, W. L., Winkenwerder, W., Hackbarth, G. M., and Krakauer, H. Effectiveness in health care. *New England Journal of Medicine* 319(18):1197–1202, Nov. 1988.

18. Relman, A. S. Assessment and accountability: the third revolution in health care. *New England Journal of Medicine* 319(18):1220–22, Nov. 1988.

19. Tarlov and others.

20. Reisenberg and Glass.

21. Brook, R. H., Avery, A. D., Greenfield, S., and others. Quality of Medical Care Assessment Using Outcome Measures: An Overview of the Method (R-2021/1-HEW). Santa Monica, CA: Rand Corporation, Aug. 1976.

22. Health Care Financing Administration. *Medicare Hospital Mortality Information: 1986* (GPO No. 017-060-00206-9). Vols. I–VII. Washington, DC: U.S. Department of Health and Human Services, Dec. 1987.

23. Health Care Financing Administration. *Medicare Hospital Mortality Information: 1987* (GPO No. 017-060-00293 to 017-060-00306-5). Vols. I–XIV. Washington, DC: U.S. Department of Health and Human Services, Dec. 1988.

24. Health Care Financing Administration. *Medicare Hospital Mortality Information: 1988* (GPO No. 0117-060-00293-0 to 017-060-00306-5). Vols. I–XIV. Washington, DC: U.S. Department of Health and Human Services, Dec. 1989.

25. Ellwood.

26. Roper and others.

27. O'Leary, D. S. *The Joint Commission's Agenda for Change.* Chicago: Joint Commission on Accreditation of Healthcare Organizations, 1987, pp. 1–10.

28. Tarlov and others.

29. Reisenberg and Glass.

30. Wennberg, J. E., Roos, N., Sola, L., and others. Use of claims data systems to evaluate health care outcomes: mortality and reoperation following prostatectomy. *Journal of the American Medical Association* 257(7):933–36, Feb. 1987.

31. Stewart, A. L., Greenfield, S., Hays, R. D., and others. Functional status and well-being of patients with chronic conditions: results from the Medical Outcomes Study. *Journal of the American Medical Association* 262(7):907–13, Aug. 1989.

32. Wells, K. B., Stewart, A. L., Hays, R. D., and others. The functioning and well-being of depressed patients: results from the Medical Outcomes Study. *Journal of the American Medical Association* 262(7):914–19, Aug. 18, 1989.

33. National Center for Health Services Research and Health Care Technology Assessment. DHHS Secretary Sullivan announces NCHSR grants totaling $4 million for patient outcome research assessment teams. *Research Activities,* special release, Sept. 11, 1989.

34. Wells, K. B., Hays, R. D., Burnam, M. A., Rogers, W., Greenfield, S., and Ware, J. E., Jr. Detection of depressive disorder for patients receiving prepaid or fee-for-service care. *Journal of the American Medical Association* 262(23):3298–3302, Dec. 1989.

35. Jencks, S. F., Daley, J., Draper, D., and others. Interpreting hospital mortality data: the role of clinical risk adjustment. *Journal of the American Medical Association* 260(24):3611–16, Dec. 1988.

36. Daley, J., Jencks, S. F., Draper, D., and others. Predicting hospital-associated mortality for Medicare patients: a method for patients with stroke, pneumonia, acute myocardial infarction, and congestive heart failure. *Journal of the American Medical Association* 260(24):3617–24, Dec. 1988.

37. Kahn, K. L., Brook, R. H., Draper, D., and others. Interpreting hospital mortality data: how can we proceed? *Journal of the American Medical Association* 260(24):3625–28, Dec. 1988.

38. Dubois, R. W., Rogers, W. H., Moxley, J. H., and others. Hospital inpatient mortality: is it a predictor of quality? *New England Journal of Medicine* 317(26):1674–80, Dec. 1987.

39. Dubois, R. W., Brook, R. H., and Rogers, W. H. Adjusted hospital death rates: a potential screen for quality of medical care. *American Journal of Public Health* 77(9):1162–66, Sept. 1987.

40. Dubois, R. W. Preventable deaths: who, how often, and why? *Annals of Internal Medicine* 109(7):582–89, Oct. 1988.

41. Department of Veterans Affairs. *Review of Mortality in VA Medical Centers, 1989.* Washington, DC: Veterans Health Services and Research Administration, Office of Quality Assurance, June 1989.

42. Anderson, G. F., and Steinberg, E. P. Hospital readmissions in the Medicare population. *New England Journal of Medicine* 311(21):1349–53, Nov. 1984.

43. Desharnais, S., Kobrinski, E., Chesney, J., Long, M., Ament, R., and Fleming, S. The early effects of the prospective payment system on inpatient utilization and quality of care. *Inquiry* 24(1):7–16, Spring 1987.

44. Roos, L. L., Jr., Cageorge, S. M., Roos, N. P., and Danzinger, R. Centralization, certification, and monitoring readmissions and complications after surgery. *Medical Care* 24(11):1044–66, Nov. 1986.

45. Farber, B. F., Kaiser, D. L., and Wenzel, R. P. Relation between surgical volume and incidence of postoperative wound infection. *New England Journal of Medicine* 305(4):200–204, July 1981.

46. Gross, P. A., Neu, H. C., Van Antwerpen, D., and Aswapokee, N. Deaths from nosocomial infections: experience in a university hospital and a community hospital. *American Journal of Medicine* 68(2):219–23, Feb. 1980.

47. Hooton, T. M., Haley, R. W., and Culver, D. H. A method for classifying patients according to the nosocomial infection risks associated with diagnoses and surgical procedures. *American Journal of Epidemiology* 11(5):556–73, May 1980.

48. Mulholland, S. G., Creed, J., Dieruff, L. A., and others. Analysis and significance of nosocomial infection rates. *Annals of Surgery* 180(6):827–30, Dec. 1974.

49. Flood, A. B., Scott, W. R., and Ewy, W. Does practice make perfect? Part I: the relation between hospital volume and outcomes for selected diagnostic categories. *Medical Care* 22(2):98–114, Feb. 1984.

50. Flood, A. B., Scott, W. R., and Ewy, W. Does practice make perfect? Part II: the relation between volume and outcomes and other hospital characteristics. *Medical Care* 22(2):115–25, Feb. 1984.

51. Flood, A. B., Scott, W. R., Ewy, W., and others. Effectiveness in professional organizations on the quality of care in hospitals. *Health Services Research* 17(4):341–66, Winter 1982.

52. Lokkeberg, A. R., and Grimes, R. M. Assessing the influence of non-treatment variables in a study of outcomes from severe head injuries. *Journal of Neurosurgery* 61(2):254–62, Aug. 1984.

53. Wennberg and others.

54. Cleary, P. D., and McNeil, B. J. Patient satisfaction as an indicator of quality care. *Inquiry* 25(1):25–36, Spring 1988.

55. Davies, A. R., and Ware, J. E., Jr. Involving consumers in quality of care assessment. *Health Affairs* 7(1):33–48, Spring 1988.

56. Delbanco, T. D., Edgman-Levitan, S., Cleary, P. D., and Roberts, M. An overview of the Picker/Commonwealth Patient-Centered Care Program. Personal communication, Boston, 1989.

57. Farr, W. *Vital Statistics: A Memorial Volume of Selections from the Reports and Writings of William Farr.* Metuchen, NJ: Scarecrow Press, 1975.

58. Caper, P. The epidemiologic surveillance of medical care. *American Journal of Public Health* 77(6):669–70, June 1987.

59. Centers for Disease Control. Mortality data from the National Vital Statistics System. *Morbidity and Mortality Weekly Report* 38(8):118–23, Mar. 1989.

60. Nightingale, F. *Notes on Hospitals.* West Strand, London: John W. Parker and Sons, 1859.

61. Cope, Z. *Florence Nightingale and the Doctors.* Philadelphia: J.B. Lippincott Co., 1958.

62. Codman, E. A. *A Study in Hospital Efficiency as Demonstrated by the Case Report of the First Five Years of a Private Hospital.* Boston: Thomas Todd Co., Printers, 1917.

63. New York Academy of Medicine, Committee on Public Health Relations. *Maternal Mortality in New York City: A Study of All Puerperal Deaths 1930–1932.* New York City: Oxford University Press, for the Commonwealth Fund, 1933.

64. Moses, L. E., and Mosteller, F. Institutional differences in postoperative death rates: commentary on some of the findings of the National Halothane Study. *Journal of the American Medical Association* 203(7):150–52, Feb. 1968.

65. Bunker, J. P., Forrest, W. H., Jr., Mosteller, F., and Vandam, L. D., editors. *The National Halothane Study: A Study of the Possible Association between Halothane Anesthesia and Postoperative Hepatic Necrosis.* Report on the National Halothane Study of the Committee on Anesthesia, National Academy of Sciences, National Research Council (U.S. Government Printing Office, 0-334-553). Bethesda, MD: National Institutes of Health, National Institute of General Medical Societies, 1969.

66. The Stanford Center for Health Care Research. *Study of Institutional Differences in Postoperative Mortality* (Pub. No. PB 250 940). Springfield, VA: National Technical Information Service, 1974.

67. The Stanford Center for Health Care Research. Comparison of hospitals with regard to the outcomes of surgery. *Health Services Research* 11(2):112–27, Summer 1976.

68. Luft and Hunt.

69. Flood and others, Does practice make perfect? Part I.

70. Flood and others, Does practice make perfect? Part II.

71. Flood and others, Effectiveness in professional organizations on quality of care in hospitals.

72. Luft, H. S., Bunker, J. P., and Enthoven, A. C. Should operations be regionalized: the empirical relation between surgical volume and mortality. *New England Journal of Medicine* 301(60):1364–69, Dec. 1979.

73. Luft, H. S., Hunt, S. S., and Maerki, S. C. The volume-outcome relationship: practice-makes-perfect or selective referral patterns? *Health Services Research* 22(2):157–82, June 1987.

74. Showstack, J. A., Rosenfeld, K. E., Garnick, D. W., and others. Association of volume with outcome of coronary artery bypass graft surgery: scheduled vs nonscheduled operations. *Journal of the American Medical Association* 257(6):785–89, Feb. 1987.

75. Riley, G., and Lubitz, J. Outcomes of surgery among the Medicare aged: surgical volume and mortality. *Health Care Financing Review* 7(1):37–47, Fall 1985.

76. Sloan, F. A., Perrin, J. M., and Valvona, J. In-hospital mortality of surgical patients: is there an empiric basis for standard setting? *Surgery* 99(1):446–54, Apr. 1986.

77. Roemer, M. R., and Friedman, J. W. *Doctors in Hospitals: Medical Staff Organization and Hospital Performance.* Baltimore: Johns Hopkins, 1971.

78. Shortell, S. M., and LoGerfo, J. P. Hospital medical staff organization and quality of care: results for myocardial infarction and appendectomy. *Medical Care* 19(10):1041–54, Oct. 1981.

79. Kelly, J. V., and Hellinger, F. J. Physician and hospital factors associated with mortality of surgical patients. *Medical Care* 24(9):785–800, Sept. 1986.

80. Luft and others, Should operations be regionalized?

81. Flood and others, Does practice make perfect? Part I.

82. Flood and others, Does practice make perfect? Part II.

83. Sloan and others.

84. Roemer and Friedman.

85. Shortell and LoGerfo.

86. Flood and others, Effectiveness in professional organizations on the quality of care in hospitals.

87. Lipworth, L., Lee, J. A. H., and Morris, J. N. Case fatality in teaching and nonteaching hospitals. *Medical Care (London)* 1:71–76a, 1963.

88. Blumberg, M. S. Comments on HCFA hospital death rate statistical outliers. *Health Services Research* 21(6):715–39, Feb. 1987.

89. Blumberg, M. S. Risk adjusting health care outcomes: a methodologic review. *Medical Care Review* 43(2):351–93, Fall 1986.

90. Rutstein and others.

91. Landefeld, C. S., Chren, M. M., Myers, A., and others. Diagnostic yield of the autopsy in a university and community hospital. *New England Journal of Medicine* 318(19):1249–54, May 1988.

92. New York Academy of Medicine, Committee on Public Health Relations, *Maternal Mortality in New York City*.

93. Eason, J., and Markowe, H. L. Controlled investigation of deaths from asthma in a hospital in North East Thames region. *British Medical Journal [Clinical Research Edition]* 294(6582):1255–58, May 1987.

94. Rothwell, R. P., Rea, H. H., Beaglehole, R., and others. Lessons from the national asthma mortality study: deaths in hospitals. *New Zealand Medical Journal* 100(821):199–202, Apr. 1987.

95. Demlo, L. K., Campbell, P. M., and Brown, S. S. Reliability of information abstracted from patients' medical records. *Medical Care* 16(12):995–1005, Dec. 1978.

96. Demlo, L. K., and Campbell, P. M. Improving hospital discharge data: lessons from the National Hospital Discharge Survey. *Medical Care* 19(10):1030–40, Oct. 1981.

97. Hsia, D. C., Krushat, W. M., Fagan, A. B., and others. Accuracy of diagnostic coding for Medicare patients under the prospective payment system. *New England Journal of Medicine* 318(6):352–55, Feb. 1988.

98. Dubois and others, Hospital inpatient mortality.

99. Jencks, S. J., Williams, D. K., and Kay, T. L. Assessing hospital-associated deaths from discharge data. *Journal of the American Medical Association* 260(15):2240–46, Oct. 1988.

100. California Medical Review, Inc. *Premature Discharge Study* (prepared for the Health Care Financing Administration). San Francisco, CA: U.S. Department of Health and Human Services, no date.

101. Jencks and others, Assessing hospital-associated deaths from discharge data.

102. U.S. Department of Health and Human Services, Public Health Service, National Center for Health Statistics. *Utilization of Short-Stay Hospitals, United States, 1985, Annual Summary* (DHHS Pub. No. [PHS] 87-1752, Series 13, No. 91). Hyattsville, MD: National Center for Health Statistics, 1987.

103. Jencks and others, Interpreting hospital mortality data.

104. Jencks and others, Interpreting hospital mortality data.

105. Sloan and others.

106. Kennedy, J. W., Kaiser, G. C., Fisher, L. D., and others. Multivariate discriminant analysis of the clinical and angiographic predictors of operative mortality from the Collaborative Study in Coronary Artery Surgery (CASS). *Journal of Thoracic and Cardiovascular Surgery* 80(6):876–87, Dec. 1980.

107. Roos, N. P., Wennberg, J. E., Malenka, D. J., and others. Mortality and reoperation after open and transurethral resection of the prostate for benign prostatic hypertrophy. *New England Journal of Medicine* 320(17):1120–24, Apr. 1989.

108. Pollack, M. M., Ruttiman, U. E., Getson, P. R., and others. Accurate prediction of the outcome of pediatric intensive care. *New England Journal of Medicine* 316(3):134–39, Jan. 1987.

109. Knaus, W. A., Draper, E. A., Wagner, D. P., and others. Evaluating outcome from intensive care: a preliminary multi-hospital comparison. *Critical Care Medicine* 10(8):491–96, Aug. 1982.

110. Knaus, W. A., Draper, E. A., Wagner, D. P., and others. An evaluation of outcome from intensive care in major medical centers. *Annals of Internal Medicine* 104(3):410–18, Mar. 1986.

111. Scheffler, R. M., Knaus, W. A., and Wagner, D. P. Severity of illness and the relationship between intensive care and survival. *American Journal of Public Health* 72(5):449–54, May 1982.

112. Flood and others, Does practice make perfect? Part II.

113. Sloan and others.

114. Stanford Center for Health Care Research, Comparison of hospitals with regard to the outcomes of surgery.

115. Blumberg, Comments on HCFA hospital death rate statistical outliers.

116. Hebel, J. R., Kassler, I. I., Mabuchi, K., and others. Assessment of hospital performance by use of death rates: a recent case history. *Journal of the American Medical Association* 248(23):3131–35, Dec. 1982.

117. Jencks and others, Assessing hospital-associated deaths from discharge data.

118. Greenfield, S., Aronow, H. U., Elashoff, R. M., and others. Flaws in mortality data. *Journal of the American Medical Association* 260(15):2252–55, Oct. 1988.

119. Iezzoni, L. I. Measuring the severity of illness and case mix. In: N. Goldfield and D. B. Nash, editors. *Providing Quality Care: The Challenge to Clinicians.* Philadelphia: American College of Physicians, 1989, pp. 70–105.

120. Gonnella, J. S., Hornbrook, M. C., and Louis, D. Z. Staging of disease: a case-mix measurement. *Journal of the American Medical Association* 251(5):637–44, Feb. 1984.

121. Young, W. W. Incorporating severity of illness and cormorbidity in case-mix measurement. *Health Care Financing Review* annual supplement, pp. 23–31, Nov. 1984.

122. Knaus, W. A., Draper, E. A., Wagner, D. P., and others. APACHE II: a severity of disease classification system. *Critical Care Medicine* 13(10):818–29, Oct. 1985.

123. Brewster, A. C., Karlin, B. G., Hyde, L. A., and others. MEDISGRPS: a clinically based approach to classifying hospital patients at admission. *Inquiry* 22(4):337–87, Winter 1985.

124. Iezzoni, L. I., Moskowitz, M. A., and Daley, J. *A Description and Clinical Assessment of the Computerized Severity Index.* Prepared for the Health Care Financing Administration under Cooperative Agreement No. 18-C-98526/1-05, Health Policy Research Consortium, July 1989.

125. Knaus and others, An evaluation of outcome from intensive care in major medical centers.

126. Pollack and others.

127. Dubois and others, Hospital inpatient mortality.

128. Dubois and others, Adjusted hospital death rates.

129. Blumberg, Comments on HCFA hospital death rate statistical outliers.

130. Blumberg, Risk adjusting health care outcomes.

131. Daley and others.

132. Jencks and others, Interpreting hospital mortality data.

133. Knaus and others, An evaluation of outcome from intensive care in major medical centers.

134. Dubois and others, Adjusted hospital death rates.

135. Dubois and others, Hospital inpatient mortality.

136. Dubois.

137. Hannan, E. L., Bernard, H. R., O'Donnell, J. F., and others. A methodology for targeting hospital cases for quality of care record reviews. *American Journal of Public Health* 79(4):430–36, Apr. 1989.

138. Department of Veterans Affairs.

139. Rutstein and others.

140. Mills, *Report on Medical Insurance Feasibility Study.*

141. Craddick.

142. Summer, S. J. Maryland's experiment with quality measures. *Business and Health* 5:14–16, 1987.

143. Health Care Financing Administration, Health Standards and Quality Bureau. *1986–1988 PRO Scope of Work.* Baltimore: U.S. Department of Health and Human Services, Nov. 4, 1985.

144. Green, M. S., Rubinstein, E., and Amit, P. Estimating the effect of nosocomial infections on the length of hospitalization. *Journal of Infectious Diseases* 145(5):667–72, May 1982.

145. Gross and others.

146. Roos and others, Centralization, certification, and monitoring readmissions and complications after surgery.

147. Roos, L. L., Roos, N. P., and Sharp, S. M. Monitoring adverse outcomes of surgery using administrative data. *Health Care Financing Review* annual supplement, pp. 5–16, Dec. 1987.

148. Haley, R. W., Culver, D. H., White, J. W., and others. The nationwide nosocomial infection rate: a new need for vital statistics. *American Journal of Epidemiology* 121(2):159–67, Feb. 1985.

149. Haley, R. W., Hooton, T. M., Culver, D. H., and others. Nosocomial infections in U.S. hospitals, 1976: estimated frequency by selected characteristics of patients. *American Journal of Medicine* 70(4):947–59, Apr. 1981.

150. Haley, R. W., Quade, D., Freeman, H. E., and others. The SENIC Project. Study on the efficacy of nosocomial infection control: summary of study design. *American Journal of Epidemiology* 111(5):472–85, May 1980.

151. Mulholland and others.

152. Britt, M. R., Schleupner, C. J., and Matsumiya, S. Severity of underlying disease as a predictor of nosocomial infection: utility in the control of nosocomial infection. *Journal of the American Medical Association* 239(11):1047–51, Mar. 1978.

153. Freeman, J., and McGowan, J. E., Jr. Risk factors for nosocomial infections. *Journal of Infectious Diseases* 138(6):811–19, Dec. 1978.

154. Anderson and Steinberg.

155. Anderson and Steinberg.

156. Desharnais and others.

157. Roos and others, Centralization, certification, and monitoring readmissions and complications after surgery.

158. Anderson and Steinberg.

159. Desharnais and others.

160. Roos and others, Centralization, certification, and monitoring readmissions and complications after surgery.

Section Three

The Introduction of Data and Their Use in Peer Review

Effective use of clinical data does not come about simply because the data are available. Medical staffs must be prepared for the data, familiar with their origins, and comfortable with their applications. In this section, chapter 5 discusses the origins of clinical data and their implications for physicians and health care institutions—issues that are critical to the credibility and uses of clinical data. Chapters 6 and 7 expand on these topics by exploring peer review from the perspective of the medical staff and the governing board, both of which share responsibility for the quality of patient care. Although these two groups carry out their respective responsibilities differently, they both need to understand how data are used in decision making.

Chapter Five

Introducing Data to Medical Staffs

William A. Schaffer, M.D., F.A.C.P.

On September 30, 1984, the system of diagnosis-related groups (DRGs) was implemented for inpatient care of Medicare beneficiaries, and all secrets of clinical outcomes died. Although attention was focused on the financial impact of DRGs, their impact on clinical practice has been equally dramatic. The computerization of clinical medicine followed, which was accomplished through the *ICD-9-CM* coding procedures, the vehicle for DRGs. Computerization allowed for common definitions of all procedures, diagnoses, and treatments for the first time.

The impact of the computerization of medicine went relatively unnoticed until March 12, 1986, when a front-page *New York Times* story[1] listed 142 hospitals with death rates higher than predicted according to an analysis of hospital mortality performed by the Health Care Financing Administration (HCFA), the payment arm of the Medicare program. It then became clear to hospitals that the data they were providing to payers using the standardized definitions permitted the comparison of mortality rates, at least among institutions.

☐ Implications of Physician-Specific and Hospital-Specific Data

Where do these data, which can be used by outsiders to judge the clinical care provided by physicians, come from? The data originate in the patient chart, the thick file of paper that is painstakingly handwritten at the patient's bedside and the nursing station. Upon a patient's discharge, the medical records staff abstracts and encodes his or her chart, which is then reviewed by a physician who signs an attestation to the validity of the codes. When the physician signs below the paragraph that reads, "I certify that the narrative descriptions of the principle and secondary diagnoses and the major procedures performed are accurate and complete to the best of my knowledge," he or she signals concurrence with the coding. The physician's signature affirms the accuracy of the diagnostic conclusions and treatments during the patient's hospital stay. Physicians must, therefore, recognize their ultimate accountability for any external perceptions of clinical outcomes after they have reviewed and signed these encoded summaries of patient care.

The attested abstracts are then sent to a payer as part of the bill for inpatient services. The hospital, the medical staff, and the physician are thereby represented to the world through these encoded medical abstract data. These data are of great importance to regulators and consumers of health care. Every clinical event has a dollar amount attached to it that is clearly identified with a diagnosis, procedure, or treatment. Payers can trace the dollars and deduce clinical outcomes. Thus, clinical outcomes can be derived from what is basically a financial system.

A tremendous pool of data is available. Computerized outcome data for the majority of the nation's inpatients reside in a handful of huge computer centers, most notably in HCFA's data center and host computer located in Baltimore, Maryland. Similar facilities exist for such major private insurers as Prudential, Aetna, and Blue Cross/Blue Shield.

Humana's strategy has been to intercept the data en route to the payer so that the data can be analyzed and returned rapidly to medical staffs for their use in internal quality management. Many medical staff members perceive this approach as an advantage in dealing with payers and regulators because they are able to see their own data first. Physicians view this approach as an early warning network that allows them to identify issues and patterns of outcomes that merit attention and analysis. Outcome data obtained in this manner and summarized for physicians across the hospital provide medical staffs with the big picture, a view of themselves as others would see them. This process is treated as an objective statistical review that impartially addresses all providers within the institution. Such a systematic, statistical review of clinical outcomes can save a large amount of time for both hospital staff and medical staff in discharging necessary quality review responsibilities.

The issue facing physicians in the 1990s, then, is not how to keep their outcome numbers secret. There will be no data secrets because information will be even more widely available and disseminated and will be extended to all customers, whether they are large-scale purchasers such as insurance companies or the federal government, state regulatory bodies, or consumer groups. Instead, physicians will face three issues in the 1990s:

- How quickly they can see their data
- How they will deal with outsiders' perceptions of their data
- How medical staffs will use and benefit from their data

☐ Issues Critical to Data Credibility

Data are worthless unless their audience believes that they are accurate and useful. Thus, medical staff orientation to clinical outcome data must make clear the origins of the data (as outlined above), the imperatives for the data's use and the risks for not using the data, and the mechanisms that ensure that the data are presented with objectivity, fairness, and validity. Once physicians understand that the coding system is not elective but is tied to reimbursement—the lifeblood of an institution—the coding process assumes a mantle of greater importance and interest. As physicians become more aware of the importance of coding and chart abstraction and gain expertise and confidence in them, the value of the clinical data recorded in abstracts improves.

Clinical data should be introduced to medical staffs cautiously, accompanied by specific education regarding the data's origin, validation, analysis, and uses. Physicians must understand that the data are accumulated on literally every clinical event in the facility and that all physicians and hospitals are treated exactly the same. The medical staff needs instruction in the validation of data entering the coding process as well as in the statistical concepts and methods governing presentation of the data analysis they receive. In addition to knowing what is done to the data, the medical staff should understand who is involved in retrieving and analyzing the data.

Data that have been factored and adjusted for severity of illness are still controversial, but unfactored, or raw, clinical outcome data have intrinsic credibility to the medical staff. To some extent, unadjusted data are well suited for use in statistical process control. In addition to gaining a clear understanding of what comprises the data, physicians learn that conclusions cannot be drawn directly from tables of data. Such tables merely identify practice patterns and trends that require further analysis. Also, physicians should be alerted to the cycle of clinical outcome reports—monthly, quarterly, semiannually, or annually—so that they can plan to incorporate them in ongoing quality reviews.

Data security is important because aggregate reports must protect physician and patient confidentiality. The end users of the data must be carefully specified. For example, policy might stipulate that a single copy of aggregate data be available for review solely by legitimate committees discussing official medical staff business. Physicians are encouraged to privately review their own data but are not allowed to review the data of others unless they are acting in an official capacity sanctioned by the medical staff committee. Because the data are the hospital's own, they can be accorded the same privilege extended to other traditional methods of properly executed peer review.

☐ Uses of Clinical Data

The most important use of the data is to *continuously improve clinical processes* in the hospital. Medical staffs cannot manage what they cannot measure, and they cannot measure without understanding basic statistical processes, such as the processes involved in determining mortality rates, morbidity rates, and frequencies of sentinel events. Lacking these statistical tools, medical staffs can only deal with clinical processes on an individual and anecdotal basis. However, with an understanding of the available statistical information, staffs can begin to analyze their performance, identify variations from desired performance, and investigate problem causes and solutions on an ongoing basis.

Another use of clinical data is in *dealing with customers*. Thresholds for clinical outcomes have been established by major third-party payers and must be met. In many cases, facilities and medical staffs must provide clinical outcome data before they are allowed to bid for group contracts. Medical staffs that can demonstrate positive outcomes will be able to attract patients in today's competitive business environment.

Maintaining institutional accreditation is another reason to develop statistical profiles of clinical outcomes. The new standards for accreditation by both Medicare and the Joint commission on Accreditation of Healthcare Organizations require that case review be subsidiary to process review. Formerly, standards could be adequately met by sequential review of individual cases that failed screens established arbitrarily by the medical staff.

In 1987, the standards were changed, with the result that cases must now be identified by reviewing the entire system, not merely by filtering cases with arbitrary screens. For example, a cardiology department cannot be adequately reviewed by medical staff members sifting through charts that failed certain thresholds. Rather, that medical staff review must encompass the entire process—the number of cases, the rate of certain medical variables, trends over time, and patterns of performance. Larger issues must be addressed, and the chart review at the individual level must result from statistical profiling. One must never draw conclusions directly from the data; instead, conclusions can be made only after individual case review.

Clinical outcome summaries can augment this process and replace the tedious manual tabulation of clinical events. Medical staffs have been receptive to these summaries and view them as a major improvement in the quality process that enables staff members to focus on targeted, intensive reviews identified through statistical analysis. Comprehensive statistical review also provides substantial time savings over manual random chart review.

Regulatory bodies also require informed action by the board of trustees. Medical staffs do not have final accountability for the quality of care in the institution; that responsibility ultimately resides with the governing board. The medical staff keeps the governing board informed of clinical quality by means of a summary management report. No longer can committee minutes be presented to the board of trustees for routine approval. Medical staffs need to provide detailed information, which is distilled statistically and meaningfully and presented to the board in executive format for management action. An analogy can be made to financial reports. For example, governing boards do not need to see individual ledger sheets for the department of respiratory therapy. Instead, they need distilled, summarized financial information that allows them to understand and draw conclusions about the department's financial performance. The same must be true of the quality process. Using sophisticated clinical outcome information, boards can understand a clinical process from statistical profiles, much as they would for any aspect of the facility's operations (see chapter 7 for further discussion of quality assurance data and governing boards).

☐ Summary

When adequately informed about the origins, implications, uses, and advantages of data, medical staffs can become active participants in the quality-of-care process and can work to improve the usefulness of the clinical data available to them. Those staffs that are suddenly confronted with "secret" numbers that have been factored or adjusted and then represented to draw conclusions about quality of care are less likely to cooperate. Such staffs will probably be justifiably cautious and suspicious of such approaches to statistical outcomes.

When clinical outcome data are used for continuous quality improvement and not for the purpose of making judgments, medical staffs that have been prepared in advance and involved in the process can become the strongest component of this approach.

Reference

1. Brinkley, J. U.S. releasing lists of hospitals with abnormal mortality rates. *New York Times,* Mar. 12, 1986, p. A.1.

Chapter Six

Quality Assurance Data Management: The Physician's Role

Jonathan T. Lord, M.D.

Medical staffs in all settings—hospitals, managed care plans, group practices, and private offices—are being confronted with the need to use outcome and other data and to transform them into meaningful information. With the dissemination to the public through national magazines and local newspapers of data on health care costs and quality (for example, the statistics and reports of mortality and morbidity rates, the frequency of and the indications for surgical procedures, and so on), physicians must be involved in the collection of such data, the accuracy of the data collection methods, the analysis of the data, and ultimately, the dissemination of the data to their institutions as well as the public. And, as a result of this involvement, physicians must also try to translate this information into actions that will result in sustained improvement in patient care.

The transformation of data into information is an essential process in the maintenance of an effective quality management program. For this process to take place, the following elements are required:

- *Clinically significant review topic(s):* those aspects of care that are significant by virtue of their volume, their risk, or the experiences of the medical staff.
- *Timely collection of data:* a procedure that moves from an environment of retrospective data collection and review toward concurrent data collection and analysis.
- *Accurate data:* the information that can be obtained from primary source documents such as physicians' orders or progress notes rather than just from "convenient" but erroneous data bases in hospital mainframe computers.
- *Functional data displays:* the visual supports that allow an "at-a-glance" analysis rather than require a lengthy study of reams of computer printout sheets.
- *Educated staff to effect data analysis:* those individuals who can provide quality management staff and medical staff leadership with the tools to perform data analysis, including basic statistics, software for data displays, and communication skills.
- *Actions to improve patient care based on the analysis of the data:* the activities that are the primary product of all quality assurance/improvement endeavors. Actions should be assessed to ensure that they have resulted in the sustained improvement in patient care.

This chapter describes important areas for data analysis, dimensions of quality management data, methods for data display and communication of results of data evaluation, and methods for involving the medical staff in data analysis. A number of practical examples of data analysis are also provided.

☐ Important Areas for Data Analysis

In the past several years the Joint Commission on Accreditation of Healthcare Organizations (Joint Commission) has set the direction for data requirements related to quality and institutional management. Its Agenda for Change[1] is shifting the focus of the accreditation process from structural and process considerations to analysis of outcomes of care. The Joint Commission has invested significant resources in the development of this project through the design and development of clinical indicators, the field-testing of these indicators at selected hospitals, and the evaluation of mechanisms for the transmittal of data from hospitals to the Joint Commission.

At the heart of the quality management process is the analysis of performance at the institutional, unit/product-line, and individual levels. At the institutional level, data elements usually involve global indicators related to quality, risk management, and utilization management. The Health Care Financing Administration (HCFA) has related mortality data on a yearly basis since 1987 in order to provide hospital performance data to the public. The Maryland Hospital Association has taken a more comprehensive approach to assessing institutional performance through its Quality Indicator Project.[2] Designed for use by governing boards, the project collects data on the following elements and provides comparative and normative data that should enhance analysis by allowing identification of outliers:

- Cesarean section rates
- Inpatient mortality
- Nosocomial infections
- Surgical wound infections
- Neonatal mortality rates
- Readmission rates
- Admissions following ambulatory surgery
- Returns to operating rooms
- Ambulatory care indicators

Unit/product-line data and analysis have frequently focused on financial performance, usually examining cost/ordering practices associated with specific diagnosis-related groups (DRGs) or some other payer categorization system. Some institutions have begun to "marry" these financial analyses with quality measures[3,4] to more effectively analyze performance within specific DRGs or by specific organizational unit (for example, the intensive care unit).

Perhaps the most difficult level on which to implement the collection and analysis of data is that of the individual practitioner. The Joint Commission[5] and regulatory agencies require a performance-based credentials review and privileging program that depends on objective information to support decisions for the delineation of clinical privileges. Many institutions have misinterpreted these requirements to mean that the entire focus of quality management programs needs to be on the performance of individual practitioners and, as a result, have created quality assurance (QA) "phobia" among members of the medical staff, who believe that efforts in quality management are designed to adversely affect physician practice. It must be emphasized that the design of systems to profile practitioner performance should do the following:

- Include all practitioners (physicians, dentists, allied health professionals and nurses), not just physicians
- Be described to all practitioners prior to implementation
- Contain data that have been subjected to the peer review process
- Be available to the practitioner when requested
- Contain balanced information, including both numerator and denominator data points

Interpretation of practitioner-specific information should take place through established peer review mechanisms and should be the primary responsibility of the chairmen of clinical departments or services.

☐ Dimensions of Quality Management Data

Assessment of performance at any level, whether institutional, unit/product-line, or individual practitioner, requires analysis along the dimensions of cost and quality.

Cost

Cost by DRG or *ICD-9-CM* code allows for the analysis of multiple variables related to resource consumption, such as length of stay (LOS), utilization of ancillary testing, product selection and practice preferences, labor intensity, and other factors. A limitation faced by many hospitals and health care organizations is the inability to accurately determine costs because of the absence of a system for patient-based cost accounting. The financial systems of most institutions capture charges that can help in the analysis of ordering practices, utilization of ancillary services, and LOS; however, analysis of total resource consumption is not possible with these types of systems.

Quality

Data for quality analysis have traditionally focused on measures of disquality—death, unplanned readmissions, returns to operating rooms, infections, medication errors, and the like. These data can be analyzed meaningfully in conjunction with cost and can be stratified at the institutional, unit/product-line, or individual practitioner levels. However, analyses of these data are subject to the caveats of data analysis.

Looking toward the future, the implementation of programs designed to continuously improve quality will require different data elements. Total quality management, reflecting the work of W. Edwards Deming,[6] approaches quality improvement through the analysis of the processes of care—that is, analysis of the manpower, methods, materials, and machines, or, stated differently, procedures, policies, people, and equipment—that go into providing a specific service (or DRG). Data elements that reflect work flow are critical to this process, followed by steps for incremental improvement in care. An example would be analysis of the following variables of care provided to patients that present to the emergency room with chest pain:

- Minimizing triage time
- Obtaining the pertinent history
- Documenting key clinical findings
- Ensuring that patients are placed on thrombolytic protocols within the appropriate time interval
- Evaluating the patient flow times from admission to special care units
- Following up on diagnostic accuracy

☐ Methods for Data Display and Communication of Results of Data Evaluation

The link between data and the transformation of data into information is usually the staff of the quality management department. The individual with primary responsibility is often the director of the quality management department or the medical director of the institution. Key to the transformation of the data is their preliminary analysis and display. Too often, data for quality management activities are contained in reams of computer printouts that are brought to meetings of clinical departments of medical staff committees without any analysis by, or prior discussion with, the chairperson or other key member of the committee.

Data Display

Data need to be presented in compact form and should be associated with visual displays that are clear, focused, and understandable, allowing for ready identification of key findings. Types of displays include the following:

- Flowcharts (used as descriptions of processes)
- Cause-and-effect diagrams (used to brainstorm factors that influence outcomes)
- Trend (run) charts (data charted over time and used to examine trends)
- Histograms (used to measure frequency of events)
- Control charts (used as continuing guides for quality improvement; contain defined upper and lower limits on either side of the average result)
- Scatter diagrams (method used for charting the relationship between two variables)
- Pareto charts (used to determine priorities; aid in the identification of the factors that "make a difference")

Figure 6-1 contains examples of each of the preceding data displays.

Communication of Results

In order for data to make the journey to information, they not only need to be packaged and displayed, but they must also be received. The reception of data requires the following:

- Participation of the end user in the design of the quality management program to ensure that data elements are relevant
- Tailoring of the data displays to requirements of regulatory agencies
- Pilot-testing of the data collection tools and clinical indicators
- Education of the end user about methods for data collection and display
- Discussion of the limitations of the data
- Preliminary presentation of data to the chairperson or key member(s) of departments or committees prior to formal presentation at meetings
- Use of feedback from the end user(s) of data to modify methods for data collection or data display

Typically, the end users of these data are the medical staff, the executive management, or the governing board of the institution. Generally, all three of these major constituent groups of the hospital require education about data management and the elements of effective quality management programs. Education is the mechanism with which to get the "receiver" involved so that the data will be used.

Figure 6-1. Types of Data Display

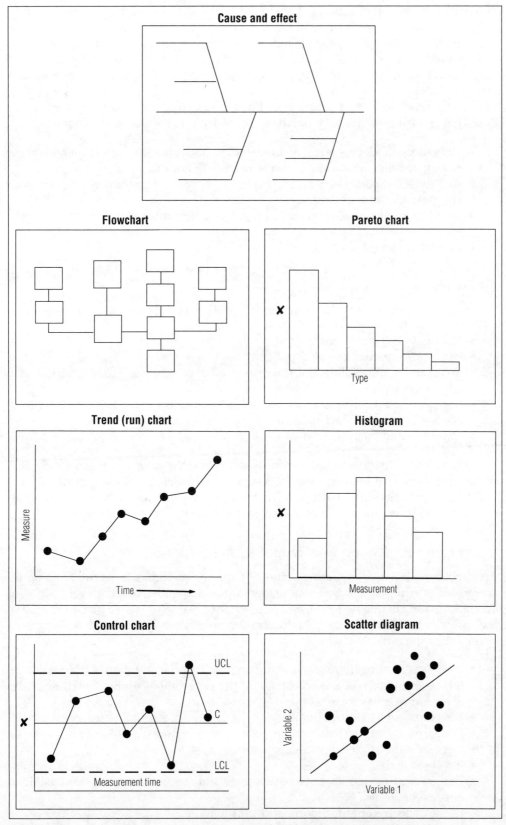

Adapted from King, B. *The Quality Management Implementation Manual Health Care Series.* GOAL, 1990.

☐ Methods for Involving the Medical Staff

The culture of the organization and the relationship of the medical staff, the administration, and the governing body are factors that determine the extent of the medical staff's participation in data analysis and use. The development of strong relationships among these bodies is critical. Participation can also be gained through education, open communication, involvement in every step of the process, and, prehaps most important, patience.

Most physicians are not naturally inclined to be active participants in these activities. Their reticence is due to a combination of factors, including the following:

- Limitations and pressures of time (office and practice commitments, home responsibilities, and administrative responsibilities to the hospital)
- Anxiety about potential repercussion of these activities (medicolegal implications and potential impact on referral patterns)
- Attachment of negative image to most QA programs (punitive impact of most programs, bureaucratic versus clinical focus of many programs)
- Lack of understanding of the "rules"

Education

Educational activities for the medical staff should be provided in the following areas:

- National health care environment
- Health care regulations and policies
- Roles and responsibilities of the organized medical staff, administration, and governing body
- Basic principles of management, including information on organizational behavior and on how to conduct meetings that motivate professionals
- Handling and analysis of data

Educational activities should be conducted through a variety of means, including attendance at external seminars and workshops, medical staff "retreats" using external facilitators, and ongoing internal educational programs and materials. Emphasis must be placed at leadership and department or committee chairperson levels.

Open Communication and Ongoing Participation

An important strategy for gaining "buy-in" from the medical staff is the ongoing involvement of educated medical staff leadership and members during every phase of the development of quality management programs, especially those phases related to the analysis of data and the communication of results. Participation should be stressed in the following critical activities:

- Design of the quality management program (special attention should focus on the needs of both the medical staff and the expectations of the governing body)
- Selection of areas for review
- Development of clinical indicators or criteria and thresholds for evaluation
- Development of mechanisms for data collection and data display
- Development of mechanisms for data analysis
- Analysis of data
- Design of actions to improve patient care and mechanisms to assess sustained improvement
- Design and routing of reports and information
- Periodic reassessment of the quality management program

Patience and Vision

Getting the full and active participation of the medical staff in quality data management will be a long-term endeavor for most institutions. In addition to the educational activities described previously, health care organizations, "organized medicine," and health care policymakers must do everything possible to eradicate the legacy of punitive connotations attached to quality assurance, risk management, and utilization review programs, which has resulted in avoidance behavior by many physicians and health care professionals in this country.

Chief executive officers, medical directors, and directors of quality management programs need to assess not only the national health care landscape, but also the environment of their medical staff and the status of their hospital's quality management program in order to realistically develop plans for the full participation of their medical staff in quality data management. Patience and vision go hand in hand in this process. Strategies should include the following:

- *Plan for incremental improvement.* Quality improvement activities should be implemented one step at a time. Hospitals and medical staffs are well served when quality improvement activities focus on doing a few things well instead of doing many things poorly.
- *Celebrate success and learn from failure.* Quality management staffs should practice what they preach by continually assessing what they do and looking for ways to do it better. Successes should be celebrated throughout the organization.
- *Provide incentives.* The needs and perspectives of the medical staff should be assessed and incentives provided. Incentives may include providing mechanisms that free up physician time, focusing quality improvement activities on the development of new programs and technologies that members of the medical staff want, or supporting clinical research programs at teaching hospitals.
- *Plan long term to ensure the full participation of the medical staff in the management, planning, and direction of the organization.* Apply strategic thinking principles to the development of quality improvement activities. Quality improvement needs to become a corporate value that is constantly tested in organizational decision making.

☐ Examples of Quality Management Data Reports and Interpretation of Their Results

Every set of data must be approached individually; none can be generalized to every institution. The following set of questions should be asked prior to data analysis:

- Are the parameters clinically relevant?
- Are there any significant statistical issues, such as sample size, that need to be taken into account?
- What is the source of the data? How were the data collected?
- Were there any significant underlying assumptions?
- What are you going to do with the data? Who needs to know?

Some real-life examples of data application and assessment follow.

Example 1

The Medicine Department of Bay Hills General Hospital received its 1989 annual report about the utilization review performance of its members (see table 6-1). The data will be included in the profiles of physician performance used at the time of reappointment.

Table 6-1. Annual Utilization Review Report

Physician	Total Denied Days	Total Inpatient Days	Adjusted Denial Rate, 1989
Smith	0	112	0%
Jones	12	1,243	0.2%
Harris	14	140	5.58%
Fran	67	612	0.45%
Reed	22	989	0.34%
Young	18	564	0%
Weeks	9	433	0.21%
Linde	0	1,123	0%

In looking at this report, the following questions need to be addressed in order to understand what the data truly mean (illustrative answers are included):

1. What constitutes a *denied day*?
   Answer: External denial of hospital charges by either the peer review organization or Blue Cross.
2. How is the *denial rate* adjusted?
   Answer: The adjusted denial rate excludes denials related to patients waiting for nursing home placement, which was outside the physician's control.

In analyzing the report, the following findings are significant:

1. Dr. Harris has a significantly different adjusted denial rate, which requires further evaluation. It is important to note that the rate alone does not indicate poor utilization, but only that additional review of the cases that contributed to the rate should be evaluated. The limited value of the adjusted denial rate as a clinically significant data element should also be noted.
2. Dr. Fran has a significantly higher number of total denied days. Consistent with the preceding discussion, a review of the relevant cases is warranted.
3. Drs. Smith and Linde have had no denied days in 1989. If this represents "good" performance, evaluation of the processes used by these physicians might help in the effort to improve quality for all the physicians in the department.

Example 2

Bay Hills General Hospital received a report of a multicenter research project designed to evaluate expected versus actual mortalities of cardiac patients (see table 6-2). The report was given to the medical director of the Coronary Care Unit. In order to understand the report, the medical director must ask the following questions (illustrative answers are included):

1. What period of time is covered?
   Answer: One year—1987.
2. Are the data accurate? What is the source of the data?
   Answer: Yes; hospital billing tapes.
3. How many and what types of hospitals were included in the study?
   Answer: 300 teaching and university-affiliated hospitals.

In analyzing the data, the following additional information would be helpful: other risk and severity-adjusting information (gender, smoking history), information about

Table 6-2. Cardiac Care Review

Admissions		Total Deaths	Expected Deaths	Mortality Rate versus Expected Rate
Total	1,120	112	56	10% versus 5%
By age				
<50	220	11	5	5% versus 2.3%
50–65	600	35	30	5.8% versus 5%
>65	300	66	21	22% versus 7%

source of the patient (emergency room, transfer in), and information about hospital services (cardiac catheterization, angioplasty). In addition, more information is required about the category of patient admissions. For example, are these acute myocardial infarction patients only or are they all chest pain admissions to the hospital? Also, what assumptions are used to determine the "Expected Deaths" category?

The data do not mean that Bay Hills is not a good hospital for cardiac care. However, they do raise the possibility that the mortality rate is high. A key element not included in the table is information about the distribution of data for all the hospitals included in the study. It is conceivable that the performance of Bay Hills is within a "normative" distribution for all hospitals studied. In addition, the above-mentioned risk and severity issues must be considered. The medical director of the Coronary Care Unit should consider reviewing the mortalities for 1987 to determine trends and may want to analyze the mortality rates for 1988 and 1989.

Example 3

Dr. Don Stone, the vice-president for Medical Affairs at Bay Hills General Hospital, receives a call from the local newspaper and is asked a series of questions regarding the recent public release of mortality data. The questions and a discussion of the appropriate responses are as follows:

- The expected range of mortalities for your hospital was 6.5 percent to 13.9 percent, and your data indicated that your mortality rate was 13.7 percent. What does that mean? Are you concerned with that "high" rate? What are you doing about it?
- In two categories, stroke and respiratory illness, why was your rate higher than the expected?
- How are these data used by the hospital?

The time to start thinking about public inquiries regarding HCFA's mortality data is when the data are first presented to the hospital in their preliminary form (usually about 30 days prior to public release). In this case, after receiving the data, Dr. Stone reviewed their accuracy and prepared a synopsis of the data and their potential implications. The synopsis was presented to the executive committee of the medical staff and the governing board prior to the newspaper's telephone call. Dr. Stone answered the questions by providing the following information:

- The hospital's performance was consistent with that of other hospitals providing the same complexity of care. The 13.7 percent rate was within the expected range. The hospital uses the data as a small part of its QA activities.
- For the specific diseases where the hospital's rate was higher than the expected range, the number of cases was so small that variations in one or two cases would significantly alter the rate.

- The hospital has a QA program that reviews each individual case and cumulative results on an ongoing basis. Thus, there were no surprises in the public data. The reported mortality figures allow for comparisons in performance on a basic level, and although the hospital looks at every category that is outside the expected range, there is no direct correlation between the data and the quality of care at the hospital.

☐ Summary

Data management for clinical quality requires effective strategies for the following:

- Quality management program design
- Data collection and display
- Ongoing education and involvement of the medical staff, the administration, and the governing body

Data systems are ultimately required to support these activities but should only be considered after a quality management program has been designed and implemented. As the quality management program is developed, thought must be given to the nature and extent to which data will be incorporated. The program must realistically address how, where, and by whom data will be collected and analyzed. Proper precautions and safeguards must be taken to ensure the data's confidentiality. Finally, the medical staff must be educated to understand how data can be used to frame questions and analyze problems.

References

1. Joint Commission on Accreditation of Healthcare Organizations. *Agenda for Change.* Vols. 1 and 2. Chicago: Joint Commission, 1988–1989.

2. Maryland Hospital Association. *Quality Indicator Project Manual for Hospitals.* Lutherville, MD: MHA, 1988.

3. Jessee, W. F. Approaches to improving the quality of health care: organizational change. *Quality Review Bulletin* 7(7):13–18, July 1981.

4. Berwick, D. M. Continuous improvement as an ideal in health care. *New England Journal of Medicine* 320(1):53–56, Jan. 5, 1989.

5. Joint Commission on Accreditation of Healthcare Organizations. *Accreditation Manual for Hospitals.* Chapter MS.6. Chicago: Joint Commission, 1990.

6. Deming's philosophy improves quality. *Hospital Peer Review* 13(10):121–24, Oct. 1988.

Chapter Seven

Quality Assurance Data Management: The Trustee's Role

Carol F. Dye

The focus of this chapter is how data can assist the board of trustees in operationalizing its role as the overseer of quality in the health care facility. The text reviews the role that data can play in the quality assurance (QA) activities of trustees and suggests guidelines that trustees can follow to manage those data, specifically, the types of data that can be utilized, the form of their submission, and the suggested responses that trustees can have to the data. Review of these issues will make it clear that the utilization of data is an intrinsic part of the overall role of trustees.

☐ Defining the Role of the Trustee in Quality Assurance

Governing boards are responsible to the community for the quality of care rendered at their institutions. They also oversee the assets and resources of the institution, many of which derive from the public itself. The responsibility of trustees for the quality of care in their health care facilities is defined by the following sources:

- The mission of the hospital or health care facility
- The public trust that is invested in the board to oversee the institution's commitment to patient safety
- The standards established by various bodies for the conduct of hospitals and the practice of medical care
- The legal decisions that are made regarding hospitals and health care
- The federal and state statutes and regulations

Boards govern through a variety of activities or functions, including the following:

- Establishing the mission of the institution
- Setting policy
- Hiring effective management
- Reviewing the plans of management and setting priorities
- Overseeing the finances of the organization

- Assessing quality, including the appointment, reappointment, and delineation of privileges of the medical staff
- Setting the tone for the organization
- Acting as liaison between the community, the medical staff, and the administration

The board's ability to oversee these functions depends on its access to timely and meaningful data. When boards are given relevant information in a form they can understand, they are in a better position to respond appropriately, that is, to review, question, and set policy in an effective manner. Providing data that are concise, appropriately displayed, and organized in a comparative format will maximize the use of the board's time and assist its members in accomplishing the aforementioned activities in an efficient and effective manner.

Boards have become adept at reviewing financial data presented in forms such as current ratios, liquidity ratios, cash flow to total debt ratios, and so forth. Thus, for the most part, trustees will be comfortable reviewing quality-of-care information presented in similar statistical formats. Other trustees may benefit from having the data put into formats such as bar graphs, pie charts, and so forth that translate the statistical information into a visual image of the institution's progress.

One associated task for trustees is the representation of the institution to the public. As hospitals are placed under increasing scrutiny by the public, the public is demanding more information about the hospitals' quality of services. These demands require quantification of quality. Because the facility's reputation can often depend on the public disclosure of data intended to measure quality, trustees must understand these measures and know how to utilize them.

☐ Operationalizing the Board's Responsibility for Quality

The key to the board's success in carrying out its responsibilities is education. This education involves understanding the institution's QA program as well as the data being generated both inside the organization and by external sources.

Review of the Quality Assurance Program

The board's education begins with a review of the institution's QA program. Answering the following questions should be part of such a review:

1. What type of coordinated program does this facility have in place to integrate the review activities of all services for the purpose of both enhancing the quality of patient care and identifying current and potential problems?
2. How are the clinical and nonclinical activities of the institution monitored, and how are these two components integrated to ensure that the QA program is comprehensive?
3. How is the hospital organized to carry out the QA program? How are the services and departments organized for this function, and how are their activities coordinated? For example, is there a QA director for each individual department or a central QA department for the entire institution?
4. To whom do the various committees concerned with aspects of QA report, and how often?
5. What are the institution's regular quality assurance and utilization review activities, and how often are they undertaken (for example, departmental review, surgical case review)?

6. What kinds of information will be reported to the board, how often, and in what form? Because boards undertake much of their activity through the committee structure, how are they organized to receive and review information? Also, which committees have board representation, for example, the quality assurance committee, the credentials committee, the joint conference committee?

The governing board should be able to infer the answers to these key questions from well-designed reports and data displays.

The board's education with regard to the QA process should not end with this general overview. As activities and assessment tools are refined, the trustees should be apprised of these changes. And, of course, new trustees will need to undergo the same process. Once the structure for monitoring has been reviewed, the next step will be to review the types of data that can be generated through both external and internal mechanisms.

Review of Data

This book provides a great deal of information about the types of data that can be generated for quality assurance as well as the process of turning that data into information. When sharing data with a board of directors, it is important to remember that few trustees are health care professionals. Thus, they may be unfamiliar with the data when first exposed to them. Careful attention should be paid to educating the trustees about certain concepts that govern data, such as validity, statistical confidence interval, sample mean, and standard deviation.

The following questions are useful in reviewing quality-of-care data with boards. Even if trustees do not ask these questions, the answers should be part of the process of orienting them to the data:

1. How were the data collected and by whom?
2. How often are data collected?
3. How large is the sample?
4. How do these data compare to data from previous assessments?
5. What do the data suggest about the quality of care? Can specific patterns be identified? Are there individual sentinel events that require action?
6. Are there other reviews that need to be undertaken in order to provide a more complete and/or accurate picture of the hospital's quality of care?
7. What should we strive for as a final goal in a particular area? What would be an appropriate objective for improvement?
8. How do we compare to other hospitals?

If the data identify any adverse trends or occurrences, trustees should ask the following questions:

1. If a problem or a potential problem emerges, what actions will be taken to correct or eliminate the problem and prevent or reduce its recurrence?
2. Is there an area (department, procedure) that requires focused review?
3. What departments and which professionals will be notified of the findings, and what role will they have in the follow-up?
4. Will a report be provided to the board or an appropriate committee of the board and at what point in time?
5. Have the problem, the review, and the plan of correction been documented?

As discussed in other chapters of this book, data alone are not information. The form in which data are presented is critical to trustees in fulfilling their monitoring responsibilities because that form allows them to visualize the institution's state of affairs. Trustees cannot take action until they can "see" what should be done. Data become information, therefore, once they are in a form that is easy to review and understand. Figure 7-1 shows a particular type of data displayed in a form that allows trustees to carry out their role.

Figure 7-1 shows the position of one hospital's mean in relation to the sample mean of a number of hospitals, with regard to 10 indicators. It not only collapses information about 10 indicators into one picture, but it also presents the information together with the statistical concepts that provide the context for interpreting the data—standard deviation, sample mean, and statistical confidence interval.

The trustees who reviewed this figure were able to see that the hospital is an outlier in two areas—perioperative mortality and rate of cesarean section. With regard to perioperative mortality, the Department of Surgery was asked to follow up with further review and report back to the board. The Department of Obstetrics had already begun an obstetrical review program on a case-by-case basis.

This figure illustrates data for one particular project in which a limited number of hospitals participated. A review of other areas of data collection follows, which further demonstrates some of the means available to trustees in the management of data.

Incident Reports

New York State requires the reporting of hospital incidents to the State Department of Health. Because these incidents are specific patient occurrences, they represent one kind of information that boards should use to monitor quality of care in their institutions. The following case example illustrates how boards can use incident reports as one component of their QA program.

Incidents that must be reported in New York State include the following:

Figure 7-1. Statistical Array of Ten Quality Indicators for One Sample Hospital

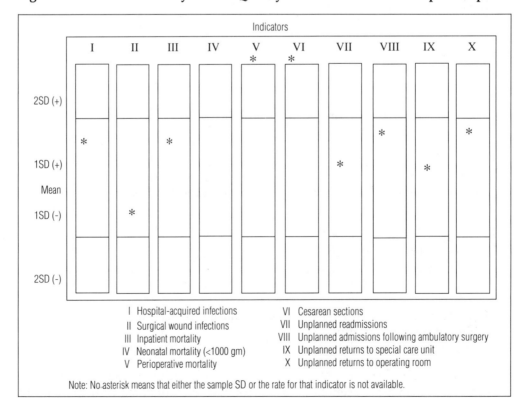

Indicators

	I	II	III	IV	V *	VI *	VII	VIII	IX	X
2SD (+)										
1SD (+)	*		*					*		*
							*		*	
Mean										
1SD (-)		*								
2SD (-)										

I Hospital-acquired infections
II Surgical wound infections
III Inpatient mortality
IV Neonatal mortality (<1000 gm)
V Perioperative mortality

VI Cesarean sections
VII Unplanned readmissions
VIII Unplanned admissions following ambulatory surgery
IX Unplanned returns to special care unit
X Unplanned returns to operating room

Note: No asterisk means that either the sample SD or the rate for that indicator is not available.

Source: Maryland Hospital Association.

- Patient deaths or impairments of bodily functions in circumstances other than those related to the natural course of illness, disease, or proper treatment in accordance with generally accepted medical standards
- Fires in the facility that disrupt the provision of patient care services or cause harm to patients or staff
- Equipment malfunction during treatment or diagnosis
- Poisoning occurring within the facility
- Strikes by facility staff
- Disasters or other emergency situations outside the hospital environment that affect health facility operations
- Termination of any services vital to the continued safe operation of the health care facility or to the health and safety of its patients and personnel

The experience of one hospital in New York demonstrates the steps a board might take in response to the opportunity to collect and utilize data. This particular hospital's QA program was called into question as a result of two patient deaths that occurred during childbirth.

Recognizing the importance of being informed of incidents that result in patient death or impairment, the board passed a resolution delineating clear policies with respect to the incident reporting system. Specifically, the board required that all incidents reportable under New York State code be investigated to identify all pertinent details needed to complete a report to the State Department of Health. Once an incident is accepted as reportable, the following individuals are to be notified: the president of the hospital, the chairperson of the QA committee, the chief of the department in question, the director of the area in which the incident occurred, the director of medical records, the medical director, the attending physician, and the consulting physician on the case, if any. Each has a role to play in developing a plan of correction, if necessary, and therefore becomes part of the system of communication to the board.

This board did not stop with the establishment of a policy; it also established a reporting structure that would give the trustees regular reports on the status of incidents—the numbers, the status of the investigation, and the types of incident (see figure 7-2). This form provides trends and allows the trustees to compare the incidents occurring in the hospital from month to month. For example, the information in the figure indicates an increase in medication errors beginning in November 1988 and dropping off in March 1989. Both the hospital staff and trustees are then able to focus on particular problem areas to determine the exact nature of the problem, how serious the problem is, where it is occurring, and so forth.

Data in the Evaluation of the Medical Staff
The system for the appointment of medical staff, the assignment of their privileges, and the monitoring and evaluation of the appropriateness of care rendered by them is one of the primary mechanisms through which the goals of quality assurance are met. For this reason, data collection for these purposes will help the board with one of its most important tasks—the approval of recommendations made by the medical staff based on demonstrated competence. This information can facilitate judgments made on the basis of objective assessment rather than through anecdote. Moreover, the presentation of these data can build a communication bridge between the medical staff and the board that allows the board to exercise its duty in a clinical area and yet not make clinical decisions.

The data should be displayed in a physician profile and divided into statistical and clinical components. For example, utilization data provided to the board should include the following:

Figure 7-2. Incident Reporting Form

Indicators	1988			1989		
	Oct.	Nov.	Dec.	Jan.	Feb.	Mar.
State reportable incidents:						
Identified by month	1	2	0	2	5	2
Current investigations	2	3	0	2	5	2
Open cases	0	9	7	9	14	11
Investigations complete	7	10	7	12	12	4
Type of occurrences:						
Medication errors	7	19	28	21	17	9
Blood and/or IV error	2	4	3	1	2	0
Patient falls	17	14	31	22	17	8
Procedure-related trauma	5	0	0	10	1	1
Equipment-related trauma	1	0	0	1	0	2
Therapy- or diagnostic procedure-related trauma	3	7	7	3	8	3
Other	3	3	9	9	7	3
Total	38	47	78	67	52	26
Risk management cases identified	0	4	0	3	0	2
Patient complaints	16	10	5	15	6	8
Department of health disability indicators:						
Temperate/short-term	1	1	0	1	5	6
Permanent/extended loss/permanent injury						
of multiple body functions/parts	0	0	0	0	0	0
Loss of life	0	1	1	2	0	0

Source: Maryland Hospital Association.

- Number of admissions
- Number of surgical procedures
- Number of outpatient visits
- Average length of stay
- Number of third-party denials
- Number of medical record suspensions
- Percentage of medical staff meetings attended
- Percentage of department meetings attended
- Percentage of committee meetings attended
- Percentage of education meetings attended
- Number of continuing medical education (CME) credits earned
- Number of disciplinary actions
- Number of professional liability claims

Clinical data reported to the board should include the following:

- Case review/evaluation (number of variances)
- Unexpected occurrences/complications (number of cases and number of variances)
- Mortality (percentage and number of variances)
- Incident reports (number of cases and variances, ranked by type of incident)
- Peer review organization review (number of variances)
- Medical record review (number of variances)
- Nosocomial infections (percentage)
- Blood utilization (number of cases and number of variances)
- Complaints (number of cases and number of variances)

- Drug/antibiotic utilization (number of variances)
- Utilization review (number of denials and number of variances)

Depending on the size of the hospital and medical staff, the board might not review each profile. The board will more likely delegate this task to the committee responsible for reviewing credentials (made up predominantly of physicians), which considers each complete profile prior to making a recommendation. Because the review of specific information concerning an individual physician occurs in that committee, boards will often delegate a trustee to sit on it.

Just as it has been considered essential that physicians be represented on the governing board and appropriate board committees, trustee representation on appropriate medical staff QA committees is also important. Having trustees on medical staff committees allows the board to have one of its own members participate in discussions. Such participation operationalizes the board oversight function at the level at which data are closely scrutinized.

Thus, not only can the board member assure his or her fellow trustees that the appropriate level of scrutiny is given, but he or she can also facilitate the review of what is often a high volume of data. Here again, the format for presentation of data becomes important when massive amounts of data are presented but only a portion of the data can be "consumed." The reappraisal summary form shown in figure 7-3 illustrates one way that data can be arrayed to expedite a sound and comprehensive review. This form allows the board or its representative to the credentials committee to determine, at a glance, whether a particular physician meets the standards for reappointment.

☐ Summary

Trustees need to recognize that quality measurement data, although moving in the direction of clearer definitions and methods, are still in a stage of development. However, the current methods of measuring quality through structure, process, outcome, and patient satisfaction, coupled with an intent to continuously improve the quality of care, can yield useful data and form a comprehensive approach to quality assurance. Systems for quality measurement require both personnel and financial support, and consideration needs to be given to the institution's technological capabilities.

The following considerations should be taken into account when attempting to increase the data literacy of the board:

- In the beginning stages, trustees will need to be educated on the existing structure for reporting and reviewing quality measurement data. Education should be provided on the entire process, and changes to the process will require additional education.
- Often the information coming to trustees will be massive in scope, detailed, and clinical in nature. Attention will need to be given by clinicians and QA staff to the presentation of data to both the medical staff and the trustees. Particular care should be taken to consolidate data in a form that can be quickly reviewed and evaluated. When possible, patterns and trends should be arrayed in a format that is visually demonstrative.
- Lack of suitable data bases, especially on a statewide and national basis, may be a barrier to comparative analysis. As the technology proliferates, this problem may be exacerbated. Therefore a concerted effort needs to be made not only to encourage such collections, but also to ensure that data are collected in similar ways to provide a basis for comparison.

Figure 7-3. Physician Reappraisal Summary

Licensure and Registration

License type: MD	Registration number: 000000	Renewal: 12/31/88	Renewal: 06/30/87
Other license:	Registration number:	Renewal:	
Attestation dates:	(1) 12/11/85 (2) 05/19/86	(3) 07/10/86 (4) 10/20/86	(5) 01/05/87

Activity and Productivity

NR admissions: 68	Consults in:	Consults out: 12	Transfers in:	Transfers out:
R admissions: 14	Consults in: 5	Consults out:	Transfers in:	Transfers out: 1
Average LOS: 23.00				
Amb Surgery Procedures: 6		OPD procedures: 12		OR procedures: 19
Prescriptions:				
Deaths: 0	Autopsies: 0	Transplants: 0		Medical examiner: 0

Quality Assurance Reviews

Review Activity	Status	Cases Reviewed	Variances	Deficiencies	Sanctions
(1) Morbidity/mortality	S	1	0	0	0
(2) Surgical case review	S	5	0	0	0
(3) Blood utilization	S	2	0	0	0
(4) Medical record review	S	3	0	0	0
(5) Infection control	S	0	0	0	0
(6) Incident reports	S	0	0	0	0
(7) Utilization review	S	1	0	0	0
(8) PRO (utilization) denials	S	4	1	1	P
(9) PRO (quality) denials	S	0	0	0	0
(10) Patient complaints	S	0	0	0	0
(11) Safety committee	S	0	0	0	0
(12) Prescription	S	0	0	0	0
(13) Medical care evaluation	S	0	0	0	0

Departmental Compliance

Departmental Committee

Committee 1 attendance rate: 1.00	Attendance rate: 1.00	Peers: S
Committee 2 attendance rate: 0.53	CME credits (1986): 8	Patients: S
Committee 3 attendance rate:	Teaching: S	House staff: S
Committee 4 attendance rate:	Other: S	Medical students: S

Reappointment Recommendations and Status

Reappointment recommendation: Y (Yes)	Medical board: Y
Peer review committee: Y	Board of trustees: Y
Credentials committee: Y	Admitting privileges: Y
Title: None	

Note: Actual profile contains identifying background information on physician such as office address(es), date of birth, other hospital affiliations, and so on.

Abbreviations: P = Pending; S = Satisfactory; R = Referred patient; NR = Nonreferred patient.

Source: *Model Hospital Board Quality Assurance Project: A Study of Trustee Involvement in Quality Assurance Management.* New York City: Hospital Trustees, June 1988. Used with permission.

- Until a suitable number of the measurement scales are put in the public domain, or until states create their own data bases, hospitals wanting comparative analysis capability may need to be part of a larger system through either purchase of a commercial software package providing such capacity or various research projects with other hospitals.
- Simply having a system in place to generate data will not minimize the ongoing need to monitor that system and its outputs. It should be recognized that management information systems will usually improve data collection but will not reduce the staffing requirement.
- When data demonstrate a hospital's patient care services to be close to the mean, there may be a tendency to make that the standard. Instead, trustees must provide the leadership needed to push toward continued improvement.

To adequately exercise their quality oversight responsibility, trustees must regularly and systematically review quality-of-care information. The benefits of data for trustees are considerable. However, these benefits will not be reaped without education, attention to presentation, and a commitment by the trustees, the medical staff, and the administration to use the data for action and change where appropriate. The opportunity to provide better care through measurable quantification can energize the hospital QA system and assure trustees that they have not only exercised their duty, but have also served their constituency—the patients and the community.

The future will provide better information that offers the hope of an improved health care delivery system. The outcome for the public will be a better health care system that maximizes the dollars spent by directing those dollars toward demonstrated quality.

Section Four

A User's Guide: Tools, Techniques, and Examples

Having dealt with fundamental issues surrounding the use, quality, and acquisition of data in the health care environment, the logical next step is to explore methods for examining the data. This inspection process is essential in the course of transforming masses of numerical facts into useful information.

In this section, a variety of basic techniques are presented that permit data to be synthesized into formats useful to health care practitioners and decision makers. Tabular, graphic, and summary measures are described. Concepts of estimation and inference are introduced, along with two well-established statistical methodologies only now gaining recognition and use in health care quality assessment and improvement: exploratory data analysis and statistical process control.

This material is not intended to replace the in-depth treatment of these topics available in the statistics literature. Rather, it is intended to introduce some basic concepts of measurement and summarization in an effort to stimulate both comfort with and interest in the inspection of statistical data.

Chapter Eight

The Inspection of Data

Randall K. Spoeri, Ph.D.

According to a quotation from Lord Kelvin, "When you can measure what you are speaking about and express it in numbers you know something about it, but when you cannot measure it, when you cannot express it in numbers, your knowledge is of a meager and unsatisfactory kind." Quality assessment and improvement requires *measurement*. Measurement enables the quantification of various aspects of health care delivery; such as clinical outcomes and resource utilization. By obtaining and examining objective measurements one may gain useful insight into and understanding of the processes under study. Measurement also provides a means of monitoring progress and conformance to standards. *Data* are the result of the measurement process. In order to use common terminology, a few definitions are needed.

The entity under study for which a measurement is made is called the *unit of analysis.* This can be a person, hospital, department, company, geographic area, time period, or other item of interest.

When the unit of analysis generates an attribute or a characteristic, this measurement is said to be a *qualitative measurement.* For example, a person who has been hospitalized can be classified as alive or dead at discharge. A hospital could be characterized as being accredited, conditionally accredited, or not accredited by the Joint Commission on Accreditation of Healthcare Organizations (Joint Commission). There must be two or more classes for the characteristic, and the classes must be mutually exclusive and exhaustive. In other words, each unit must be able to be placed in one, and only one, class. Basically, when the measurement is a *word*, this yields *qualitative data.*

When the unit of analysis generates a count, or numerical measurement on some continuum, this measurement is said to be a *quantitative measurement.* To illustrate, a person who has been hospitalized has his or her length of stay recorded in days. A hospital keeps its daily census. In general, when the measurement is a *number*, this results in *quantitative data.*

A qualitative or quantitative property that is possessed by all units of analysis but differs from unit to unit is called a *variable.* In the previous illustration a person who has been hospitalized could have two variables:

- Status at discharge (with two possibilities: alive, dead)
- Length of stay (with numerous potential values: 0, 1, 2, . . . days)

Similarly, a hospital could have two variables:

- Joint Commission accreditation status (with three possibilities: accredited, conditionally accredited, not accredited)
- Daily census (with many potential values: 0, 1, 2, . . . patients)

When measurements are collected over regular intervals of time, they are said to be *time-dependent data.* That is, the unit of analysis is a time period. To illustrate, if length of stay is aggregated or summarized by month, its measurement provides monthly time-dependent data. Similarly, a hospital's daily census is time-dependent. However, time dependency applies to qualitative as well as quantitative data. For example, a hospital's daily discharge status data (that is, the number of patients discharged alive and the number of patients discharged dead) arise from a qualitative measurement. The data can then be aggregated into monthly, quarterly, or annual summaries and examined over time.

Data are also categorized on the basis of whether they represent the complete collection of all units to be studied—a *population*—or are some part of a whole—a *sample.* (The concepts of population and sample were introduced in chapter 1.) A population is the total collection of data for all units of analysis constituting the focus of the data collection effort. A sample is a data set obtained from a part or subset of the population. A goal of many statistical studies is to draw conclusions or inferences about a populaton using a sample. When considering summary measures and techniques of estimation and inference later in this chapter, the distinction between *population data* and *sample data* will be important.

The actual differentiation between a population and a sample is, however, somewhat conceptual. For example, if data have been collected on all the patients treated in a certain hospital during a given time period, and if that hospital and time period were the sole focus of the study, the data would represent a population. On the other hand, these same data would have to be considered only a sample (and not necessarily representative of the population) if the scope of the study were regional, national, or covered a broader time period. (Sampling issues were covered in chapter 1 and therefore will not be discussed here.)

☐ Preliminary Screening of Data

Before presenting data from a population or a sample, it is important to perform some preliminary screening operations. Raw, unprocessed data obtained directly from the units of analysis under study often contain problems that should be addressed prior to any further manipulation. For example:

- If the measurement is quantitative and can be recorded with decimal places (for example, some diagnostic laboratory test result), how many places of accuracy will be retained? Consistency is important.
- Are there questionable measurements that need to be verified? For example, has a transposition of digits changed a 19-day length of stay to a 91-day length of stay? Or was a hysterectomy patient 25 years old or 52 years old? Often called *outliers,* such anomalous data items first need to be identified and then verified or corrected or even removed, as they can be highly influential in the analysis.
- What if measurements are not available for each unit of analysis? This *missing data* scenario occurs with regularity. A protocol for handling missing data needs to be developed and applied.

Once the raw data have been carefully scrutinized and answers have been obtained to questions such as those above, the data can be organized for presentation.

☐ Tabular Presentation

The following is a discussion of the presentation of qualitative and quantitative data in tabular format.

Qualitative Data

Summarizing and presenting qualitative data in a tabular format is relatively easy to do and potentially very useful. As mentioned previously, qualitative measurements are attributes or characteristics possessed by each unit of analysis.

The first step is to list the possible categories for the variable of interest. For example, suppose one is looking at the charts for 200 surgical patients discharged from a particular hospital, and the variable of interest is their status at discharge—whether they were alive or dead. The number in each category could be tallied and the data presented in a *one-way table* (that is, a table in which only one characteristic is being tabulated), as illustrated by table 8-1.

Qualitative variables can also result in more than two categories. These measurements can similarly be tallied and the percentages in each category tabulated. To illustrate, suppose in the preceding example the Uniform Hospital Discharge Data Set (UHDDS) definitions of discharge status were applied:

- Discharged to home
- Discharged against medical advice (AMA)
- Discharged to another short-term hospital (STH)
- Discharged to a long-term care (LTC) institution
- Died
- Other

If the previous 200 patients were further classified in this way, an alternative one-way tabular display would result (see table 8-2).

Two-way tables and *multiway tables* can also be prepared when the units under consideration are tabulated using two or more qualitative variables simultaneously. For example, suppose there are two qualitative variables: status at discharge (alive or dead) and day of admission (weekday or weekend). If a particular hospital had 1,064 admissions in one month, these data could be arranged in a two-way table (see table 8-3).

Quantitative Data

Tabular displays of quantitative data are called *frequency distributions*. For the sake of illustration, table 8-4 supposes that the following data have been gathered: length of stay (LOS) in days for all the Medicare patients in a particular diagnosis-related group (DRG) for a certain hospital during one year. As can be seen, there are 58 patients having stays of varying length. In the table's present format the data are difficult to interpret, and some summarization is necessary.

The individual LOS values could be organized into what is often called an *ungrouped frequency distribution*. This tabular display is just a tally of the number of unique LOS values present in the data set. An ungrouped frequency distribution of the data introduced in table 8-4 is shown in table 8-5.

Often, an ungrouped frequency distribution will provide an adequate summary. Unfortunately, in this case the degree of summarization is still insufficient, because there is a large number of LOS categories (14) and the frequency patterns are not well defined (except for the LOS of 6 days, which occurs 11 times). Hence, a *grouped frequency distribution* is indicated. A grouped frequency distribution is a tabular presentation in which the data are organized into a certain number of classes of a particular width. Five basic steps are involved in the construction of a grouped frequency distribution:

Table 8-1. Tabulation of One Qualitative Variable

Status at Discharge	Number of Patients	Percentage of Patients
Alive	196	98
Dead	4	2
Total	200	100

Table 8-2. Alternative Tabulation of One Qualitative Variable

Status at Discharge	Number of Patients	Percentage of Patients
Discharged to home	158	79
Discharged AMA	2	1
Discharged to another STH	8	4
Discharged to an LTC institution	28	14
Died	4	2
Other	0	0
Total	200	100

1. *Determine the number of classes to use:* The number of classes usually falls between 5 and 15 and depends on the number of data items to be tabulated. A trial and error approach can generally be used to select a reasonable number of classes. The rule of thumb proposed by Sturges is still a good starting point.[1] Let k be the number of class intervals and n the number of data items to be classified.

Sturges's rule suggests that

$$k = 1 + 3.3 \log_{10}(n)$$

where $\log_{10}$ is the usual base 10 logarithm.

For the data in table 8-4,

$$n = 58$$
$$\log_{10}(58) = 1.7634$$

So

$$k = 1 + 3.3(1.7634) = 6.82$$

Thus seven classes are indicated.

2. *Calculate the class width:*

Let

max = the largest value in the data set
min = the smallest value in the data set

Table 8-3. Simultaneous Tabulation of Two Qualitative Variables

Status at Discharge	Day of Admission Weekday	Weekend	Totals
Alive	790	253	1,043
Dead	12	9	21
Totals	802	262	1,064

Table 8-4. Length of Stay for Patients in DRG XXX for Hospital Y during 19ZZ

Patient	LOS (in days)	Month		Patient	LOS (in days)	Month
1	3	Jan.		30	4	
2	6			31	7	
3	13			32	10	
4	8			33	12	
5	11	Feb.		34	9	Aug.
6	8			35	14	
7	3			36	4	
8	6			37	3	
9	9	Mar.		38	8	
10	8			39	10	
11	6			40	5	
12	9			41	5	Sept.
13	5	Apr.		42	10	
14	8			43	4	
15	4			44	4	
16	7			45	7	
17	8			46	6	
18	12			47	7	Oct.
19	6	May		48	6	
20	2			49	5	Nov.
21	6	June		50	3	
22	9			51	8	
23	9			52	8	
24	6			53	6	
25	5			54	5	Dec.
26	7			55	2	
27	3	July		56	7	
28	6			57	3	
29	4			58	6	

Then

$$\text{width} = \frac{\text{max} - \text{min}}{k}$$

For the data in table 8-4,

$$\text{max} = 14$$
$$\text{min} = 2$$

Table 8-5. Ungrouped Frequency Distribution for the LOS Data Introduced in Table 8-4

LOS	Frequency
1	0
2	2
3	6
4	6
5	6
6	11
7	6
8	8
9	5
10	3
11	1
12	2
13	1
14	1
	58

So

$$\text{width} = \frac{14 - 2}{7}$$

$$= 1.71$$

which one can arbitrarily choose to round to 2.

3. *Construct the class intervals:* Because the minimum value is 2 and the class width is 2, the first class could be "1 but less than 3 days," the next "3 but less than 5 days," and so on to "13 but less than 15 days." This selection of intervals is clearly dependent on the class width chosen in step 2, but the starting value is somewhat arbitrary. One must be careful, however, to be sure that the classes do not overlap and that they include all the data items to be tabulated.

4. *Tally the data values in each class:*

LOS Class (in days)	Tally
1 but less than 3	ΙΙ
3 but less than 5	ⅬⅣ ⅬⅣ ΙΙ
5 but less than 7	ⅬⅣ ⅬⅣ ⅬⅣ ΙΙ
7 but less than 9	ⅬⅣ ⅬⅣ ΙΙΙΙ
9 but less than 11	ⅬⅣ ΙΙΙ
11 but less than 13	ΙΙΙ
13 but less than 15	ΙΙ

5. *Produce the final frequency distribution table:* In this distribution the tallies are summarized into a column called *frequency,* and the proportion of the total in each class is called *relative frequency* (see table 8-6). A relative frequency is obtained by dividing the corresponding class frequency by *n,* the total number of data items tabulated. In this tabular presentation the number of classes is more manageable, and the frequency pattern is better defined.

Table 8-6. Grouped Frequency Distribution for the LOS Data Introduced in Table 8-4

LOS Class	Frequency	Relative Frequency
1 but less than 3 days	2	.0345
3 but less than 5 days	12	.2069
5 but less than 7 days	17	.2931
7 but less than 9 days	14	.2414
9 but less than 11 days	8	.1379
11 but less than 13 days	3	.0517
13 but less than 15 days	2	.0345
	58	1.0000

☐ Graphic Display Techniques

The following sections examine a few of the most commonly used graphic display techniques for qualitative and quantitative data—bar chart, pie chart, histogram, polygon, and line graph.

Qualitative Data

Two of the most commonly used graphic displays for qualitative data are the *bar chart* and the *pie chart*. To examine these two display techniques, data will be used from the 1988 edition of *Hospital Statistics*, published by the American Hospital Association. Table 8-7 provides a categorization of the 5,810 U.S. short-term general hospitals (that is, those whose length of stay is less than 30 days) into five "type of control" categories: not-for-profit (nongovernment), for-profit, local government, state government, and federal government.

This information is graphically displayed in a bar chart in figure 8-1. The five classes are displayed on the horizontal axis, while the vertical axis gives the number of hospitals in each class. Because the control categories are distinct, the bars are not connected.

A different way of looking at the same data is through a pie chart (see figure 8-2). A pie chart portrays each class as a "piece" of the pie, that is, as a fraction of the whole. Details on how to construct a pie chart will not be given here; however, microcomputers readily produce such graphics, and many texts on business statistics give guidance on pie chart construction.[2]

Generally speaking, a bar chart is used when one wishes to display and compare the relative magnitudes of the measurements for each of the categories under consideration. A pie chart is used when the "whole" is to be portrayed as the component parts, where the proportion of each category is of interest. However, the choice is still somewhat a matter of personal preference.

The bar chart is also an appropriate graphic display if the data are of a time-dependent nature. Suppose the quarterly mortality rate at a particular hospital for the past two years is as shown in table 8-8. A bar chart representing these data is shown in figure 8-3. This hospital's mortality rate has been steadily increasing over the past eight quarters and may indicate the need for review.

Quantitative Data

To graph quantitative data, the first step is to summarize the data into a frequency distribution. The LOS data presented earlier in this chapter (see table 8-6) will be used for this purpose.

Table 8-7. U.S. Short-Term General Hospitals by Type of Control

Type of Control	Number of Hospitals
Not-for-profit	3185
For-profit	795
Local government	1427
State government	98
Federal government	305
	5810

Source: *Hospital Statistics*, 1988 Edition. Chicago: American Hospital Association, 1988, p. 8.

Figure 8-1. Bar Chart of U.S. Short-Term General Hospitals by Type of Control

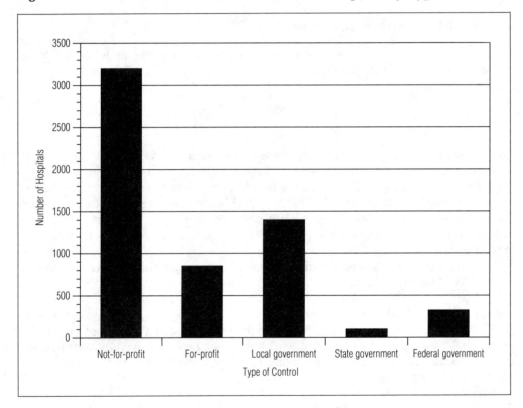

A *frequency histogram* is a commonly used graphic display of frequency distribution data. Figure 8-4 is a frequency histogram for the data shown in table 8-6. The horizontal axis contains the LOS classes, shown as a continuum. The vertical axis displays frequency. Notice that the vertical bars are connected because the LOS measurement is quantitative and continuous. This is an important difference between a bar chart and a histogram. In a bar chart the bars are *not* connected, in a histogram they *are* connected.

Sometimes *relative frequency* is displayed on the vertical axis. This is purely a matter of taste because the net result is identical to that using ordinary frequency. It is useful, however, in displaying the percentage of units falling into each class.

An alternative to a frequency histogram is a *frequency polygon* (see figure 8-5). A frequency polygon is very similar to a histogram in that the frequency distribution is its basis. The difference is that a polygon is a line graph of the frequency in a particular class versus the class midpoint. The LOS data put in the format for a frequency

Figure 8-2. Pie Chart of U.S. Short-Term General Hospitals by Type of Control

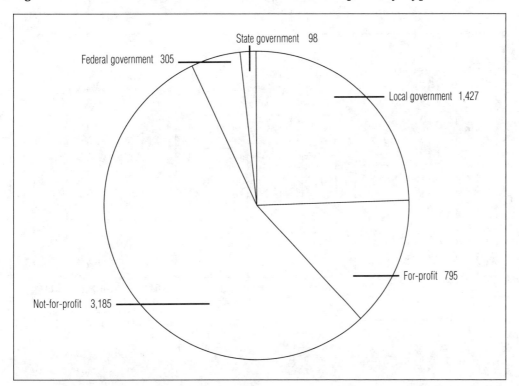

Table 8-8. Quarterly Mortality Proportion for Hospital X, 198Y–198Z

Time Period	Proportion
Q1/8Y	.0215
Q2/8Y	.0230
Q3/8Y	.0250
Q4/8Y	.0283
Q1/8Z	.0282
Q2/8Z	.0342
Q3/8Z	.0361
Q4/8Z	.0388

polygon are given in table 8-9. In this way, the midpoint is used to represent all the units in that class. A plotting convention is to "tie" the polygon at frequency (or relative frequency) zero at the midpoint in the class preceding and following the data, in figure 8-5 at 0 and 16.

Finally, suppose there are time-dependent data arising from a quantitative measurement, such as the aforementioned LOS data, which were originally organized by month. If the average length of stay (ALOS) in each month were to be calculated by summing the individual lengths of stay and then dividing the sum by the number of stays in that month, the result would be time-dependent data (see table 8-10). A line graph of these data is shown in figure 8-6. This graph conveys both the time-dependent nature of the data and the variability of ALOS over time.

These are a few of the most common of the many graphic display techniques available. A number of texts are available that discuss this topic in greater detail.[3–5] It should also be noted that the widespread availability of mainframe and personal computers simplifies the production of these and a host of other graphic displays of statistical data.

Figure 8-3. Bar Chart Displaying Time-Dependent Data from Table 8-6

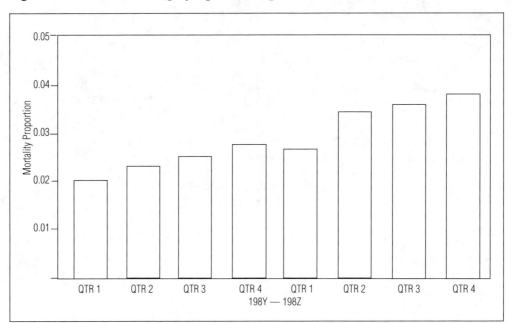

Figure 8-4. Frequency Histogram of LOS Data from Table 8-6

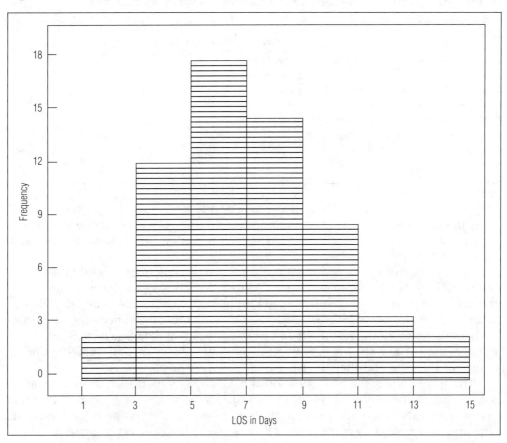

Figure 8-5. Frequency Polygon of LOS Data

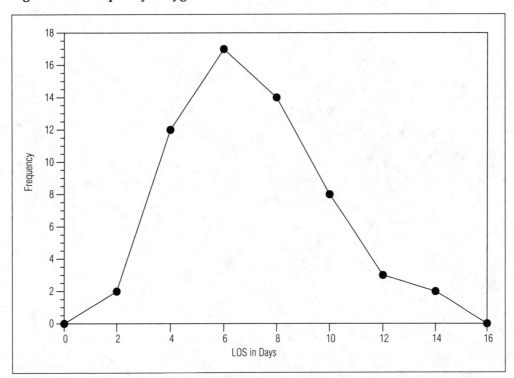

Table 8-9. Data for Frequency Polygon from Table 8-6

LOS Class Midpoint	Frequency
2	2
4	12
6	17
8	14
10	8
12	3
14	2
	58

Table 8-10. Average Length of Stay (ALOS) in DRG XXX by Month for Hospital Y, 19ZZ

Month	ALOS
January	7.50
February	7.00
March	8.00
April	7.33
May	4.00
June	7.00
July	6.57
August	7.57
September	6.00
October	6.50
November	6.00
December	4.60

Figure 8-6. Line Graph of Quantitative Time-Dependent Data from Table 8-10

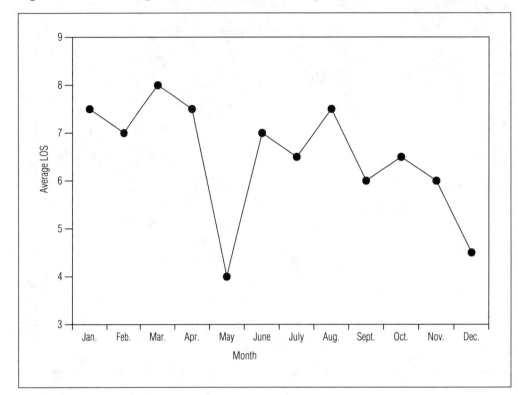

Conclusion

A word or two of caution is in order. Although tremendously useful when used properly, graphic displays are regularly misused through both intent and lack of understanding. Intent can include consciously changing the scale of measurement in midaxis (*x* or *y,* or both) to make small differences look large or vice versa. Lack of understanding can result from naively trying to present too much information in a single graphic. It is therefore always wise to examine graphic presentations of data both cautiously and critically. Several books and articles have been written that address the issue of the misuse of graphic display techniques.[6-8]

☐ Summary Measures

Having scrutinized and synthesized data into tabular and graphic formats, one may want to further distill the data into a few well-chosen numerical summary measures. These fall into three basic classes:

- Measures for quantitative data
- Measures for qualitative data
- Other measures

Data may represent a population or a sample. For brevity, this discussion will assume that the data represent a sample. Most summary measures are computed in basically the same way for populations, except that the full set of data is used. However, as full populations are infrequently used, population measures will not be discussed here. Techniques for generating summary measures from population data are discussed in a number of books.[9-12]

Measures for Quantitative Data

For consistency's sake, data will be considered in one of two formats: *individual measurements* or a *grouped frequency distribution*.

A quantitative variable X can be thought of as generating n individual measurements from a sample of n units of analysis. These n measurements will be represented in the following way:

$$X_1, X_2, \ldots, X_n$$

However, if the n measurements have previously been organized into a grouped frequency distribution, the data will be represented in the following way:

Class #	Frequency	Midpoint
1	f_1	m_1
2	f_2	m_2
.	.	.
.	.	.
.	.	.
k	f_k	m_k

Two characteristics of quantitative data sets define the major categories of summary measures—*central tendency* (or *central location*) and *variability* (or *dispersion*).

Central Tendency Measures

Knowing how a data set is "centered" is usually the first topic of interest in summarizing a data set. The purpose of a measure of central tendency is to understand where the "middle" of a set of measurements is located. However, there are several central tendency measures. Three will be described here: mean, median, and mode.

Mean

The mean is simply the *arithmetic average* obtained by adding the measurements in a data set and dividing the sum by the number of measurements. Notationally, let

$$\mu \text{ (Greek letter mu)} = \text{population mean}$$
$$\overline{X} \text{ (X bar)} = \text{sample mean}$$

For individual measurements $\overline{X}$ is found using the following formula:

$$\overline{X} = \frac{X_1 + X_2 + \cdots + X_n}{n}$$

$$= \frac{\Sigma X}{n}$$

In this formula Σ is the summation notation to indicate adding the values for the variable or expression that follows, beginning with subscript 1 and ending with subscript n.

Example: In the LOS data described in table 8-4, the $n = 6$ individual stays in June were 6, 9, 9, 6, 5, and 7 days.

That is,

$$X_1 = 6$$
$$X_2 = 9$$
$$X_3 = 9$$
$$X_4 = 6$$
$$X_5 = 5$$
$$X_6 = 7$$

So

$$\overline{X} = \frac{6 + 9 + 9 + 6 + 5 + 7}{6}$$

$$= \frac{42}{6}$$

$$= 7 \text{ days}$$

If the data under study are in a grouped frequency distribution, the following formula is used to calculate $\overline{X}$:

$$\overline{X} = \frac{f_1 m_1 + f_2 m_2 + \cdots + f_k m_k}{n}$$

$$= \frac{\Sigma fm}{n}$$

where $n = \Sigma f$.

It should be noted that this is only an approximation for the real mean of the n measurements. Because the measurements have been grouped into classes, and if the original measurements are not available, the *actual* mean cannot be computed. Therefore, the midpoint in each class is used to represent each of the measurements contained in the class. This is an assumption of necessity. If the original measurements are available, it is best to use them in calculating numerical summary measures.

Example: The n = 58 LOS measurements were arranged in a grouped frequency distribution in table 8-6. Even though all the original measurements are available, those grouped data will be used to illustrate the calculation of $\overline{X}$. (These calculations are shown in table 8-11). Had the mean been obtained from the 58 original measurements, the result would have been $\overline{X}$ = 6.64 days. Consequently, the approximate method using grouped data slightly overestimates the true mean.

The mean is a widely known and extensively used measure of central tendency. It is relatively easy to compute, uses all the data in its computation, and has useful properties for subsequent statistical inference. As such, it is regularly used in the process of inspecting data. On the downside, it is very sensitive to extremes or outliers. A few very large or small measurements can affect the value of the mean considerably. In situations such as this, the median may be a preferred measure.

Median
The median is a number that *divides an ordered array of data into two equal parts.* As such, it is the middle value, where half the data set is larger in numerical value and the other half is smaller. For individual measurements the median is obtained as follows:

Table 8-11. Calculation of $\overline{X}$ from LOS Data in Grouped Frequency Distribution Format

LOS Class	Frequency (f)	Midpoint (m)	fm
1 but less than 3	2	2	4
3 but less than 5	12	4	48
5 but less than 7	17	6	102
7 but less than 9	14	8	112
9 but less than 11	8	10	80
11 but less than 13	3	12	36
13 but less than 15	2	14	28
	58 = n		410 = Σfm

$$\overline{X} = \frac{\Sigma fm}{n}$$

$$= \frac{410}{58}$$

$$= 7.07 \text{ days}$$

1. Arrange the data set in ascending or descending order by size of measurement.

2. If n is *odd*, calculate the position $(n + 1)/2$. The measurement having this position in the ordered array is the median. If n is *even*, calculate the two positions $n/2$ and $(n/2) + 1$. Find the two measurements corresponding to these positions and average them. This average is the median.

   Regardless of whether n is even or odd, this procedure generates a median that will have half the measurements above and below it.

Example: For the LOS data in table 8-4, June had $n = 6$ measurements and July had $n = 7$ measurements:

$$\text{June: } 6, 9, 9, 6, 5, 7$$
$$\text{July: } 3, 6, 4, 4, 7, 10, 12$$

These data are placed in ascending order:

$$\text{June (ordered): } 5, 6, 6, 7, 9, 9$$
$$\text{July (ordered): } 3, 4, 4, 6, 7, 10, 12$$

For June $n = 6$ is even, so $n/2 = 3$ and $(n/2) + 1 = 4$. The third and fourth ordered measurements are 6 and 7, respectively. Hence for June the median LOS = 6.5 days. For July $n = 7$ is odd, so $(n + 1)/2 = 4$. The fourth ordered measurement is 6, so for July the median LOS = 6.0 days.

Now suppose the data are in the form of a grouped frequency distribution. Here, the following formula is used:

$$\text{median} = L + \frac{c}{f}w$$

where

L = lower-class limit of the *class containing the median* (that is, the class where the $(n/2)$th ordered data value falls, not being concerned whether n is odd or even)

c = a count of the number of measurements remaining until the $(n/2)$th measurement (the median) after L is reached in the ordered array

f = frequency in the class containing the median

w = width of the class containing the median

$n = \Sigma f$

Example: Find the median for the following grouped LOS data:

LOS Class	Frequency	Cumulative Frequency
1 but less than 3 days	2	2
3 but less than 5 days	12	14
5 but less than 7 days	17	31
7 but less than 9 days	14	45
9 but less than 11 days	8	53
11 but less than 13 days	3	56
13 but less than 15 days	2	58
	58 = n	

$n/2 = 58/2 = 29$.

The 29th value falls in LOS class 5 to 7 (the median class).

Then using our previous notation,

$$L = 5$$
$$c = 29 - 14 = 15$$
$$f = 17$$
$$w = 2$$

So

$$\text{median} = L + \frac{c}{f}w$$

$$= 5 + \frac{15}{17}(2) = 6.76 \text{ days}$$

Again, because grouped data are being used instead of the original measurements, this approach to obtaining the median is only approximate.

The median is a very useful measure of central tendency, especially because, being a *positional* measure, it is not affected by extremes. Unfortunately, the median lacks certain theoretical statistical properties, which limits its use in statistical inference. Thus, it is not as widely used as the mean.

Mode

The mode is the *most frequently occurring value* in a collection of measurements. However, by its very definition, for any given data set:

- The mode may not exist (that is, there may be none).
- The mode may not be unique (that is, there may be more than one).
- The mode may not be reflective of the central tendency of the data set.

To illustrate each possibility for individual measurements, consider the following:

Example: Suppose the number of emergency admissions per day at a particular hospital is being examined. During the first week of the study the numbers were:

$$2, 1, 5, 3, 6, 4, 0$$

There is no mode in this case because no value occurred any more often than any other. The next week saw the following results:

$$4, 2, 2, 1, 1, 5, 3$$

In this case there are two modes: 2 and 1. Furthermore, 2 and 1 are not reflective of the central location of the data.

For data in a grouped frequency distribution, the modal class is defined as the class having the largest frequency. The mode can then be taken as the modal class midpoint. For the grouped LOS data, the modal class is 5 to 7, so the mode can be taken to be 6.

Because of its obvious limitations, the mode is the least useful of the three measures of central location.

Variability Measures

Measures of central tendency alone are generally not sufficient because of the need to depict variability, or dispersion. For instance, a large variation in LOS within a particular DRG can be reason for investigation into the cause(s). To illustrate, again consider the LOS data introduced in table 8-4 and refer to the individual measurements for July and October. Computing the mean LOS for these two months yields:

$$\overline{X}_7 = 6.57 \text{ days}$$
$$\overline{X}_{10} = 6.50 \text{ days}$$

On the surface, based on only the means above, one would be tempted to conclude that these two months were quite similar. However, suppose the median were also obtained:

$$\text{median}_7 = 6.00 \text{ days}$$
$$\text{median}_{10} = 6.50 \text{ days}$$

Hence, the same conclusion would still be suggested. Suppose a relatively simple measure is first used to look at the spread of these measurements within each month.

Range

For a given data set, let

$$X_{max} = \text{the largest measurement}$$
$$X_{min} = \text{the smallest measurement}$$

Thus, the *range* can be defined as

$$R = X_{max} - X_{min}$$

For the two months, we find the following. For July:

$$X_{max} = 12$$
$$X_{min} = 3$$
$$R = 12 - 3 = 9 \text{ days}$$

For October:

$$X_{max} = 7$$
$$X_{min} = 6$$
$$R = 7 - 6 = 1 \text{ day}$$

Hence, although the measures of central tendency were quite similar, it is clear that the LOS distribution of the two months is different.

Variance and Standard Deviation

The range is useful for a first look at the variation in a set of data. However, it is necessarily affected by extremes, as it is specifically computed from only the extremes (the maximum and minimum) of a data set. Consequently, it is necessary to have a measure that is not so sensitive to extremes and also uses the entire data set. The *variance* and the *standard deviation* provide this sort of measure.

Notationally, it is conventional to use the following symbols to represent the variance:

σ^2 (Greek sigma squared) = population variance
S^2 (S squared) = sample variance

As stated before, it is assumed that sample data are being summarized. Again, we need to distinguish between data in the form of individual measurements and data in a grouped frequency distribution. If the data are individual measurements, S^2 could be found using the following formula:

$$S^2 = \frac{(X_1 - \overline{X})^2 + (X_2 - \overline{X})^2 + \cdots + (X_n - \overline{X})^2}{n - 1}$$

$$= \frac{\Sigma(X - \overline{X})^2}{n - 1}$$

where

$$\overline{X} = \text{the arithmetic mean}$$

$$= \frac{\Sigma X}{n}$$

Often called the *definitional formula*, this formula for S^2 illustrates that the variance is a composite of the squared deviations of the individual Xs from $\overline{X}$, their common mean. The divisor $(n - 1)$ performs a type of averaging of these squared deviations and is one less than n to make S^2 an *unbiased estimator* of σ^2. If the data represented a population, the sum of the squared deviations would be divided by the number of measurements without subtracting one.

The following is a useful *computational formula*, which is algebraically equivalent to the previous formula:

$$S^2 = \frac{(X_1^2 + X_2^2 + \cdots + X_n^2) - \dfrac{(X_1 + X_2 + \cdots + X_n)^2}{n}}{n - 1}$$

$$= \frac{\Sigma X^2 - \dfrac{(\Sigma X)^2}{n}}{n - 1}$$

As S^2 has been computed by squaring the original Xs, its units are squared (that is, days squared, dollars squared, and so on), which are not comparable with $\overline{X}$. For this and other technical reasons, the standard deviation is defined as follows:

$$\text{standard deviation} = + \sqrt{\text{Variance}}$$

Or

$$S = \sqrt{S^2}$$

Because the variance is *always nonnegative* (that is, $S^2 \geq 0$), this computation is always feasible, and S is in units of the original Xs (that is, days, dollars). The use of $\overline{X}$ and S together will be introduced later in this section and again in the section on statistical inference.

Example: The LOS Data for June are used to illustrate the computation of S^2 for individual measurements. The calculations are shown in table 8-12, where $n = 6$. Note that the $(X - \overline{X})$ column sums to zero. This is *always* the case, as can be proven algebraically. Note also that squaring the deviations removes the negative signs and provides a nonnegative measure of variation from the mean.

In this case the definitional and computational formulas were both easy to apply and gave exactly the same result. However, when $\overline{X}$ is not a whole number, use of the definitional formula can become tedious. Naturally, personal computers and even many hand-held calculators make these "by-hand" calculations generally unnecessary.

If the data are in the form of a grouped frequency distribution, using the previously defined notation, the definitional formula for S^2 is as follows:

$$S^2 = \frac{f_1(m_1 - \overline{X})^2 + f_2(m_2 - \overline{X})^2 + \cdots + f_k(m_k - \overline{X})^2}{n - 1}$$

$$= \frac{\Sigma f(m - \overline{X})^2}{n - 1}$$

where

$$\overline{X} = \frac{\Sigma fm}{n}$$

The computational formula is as follows:

$$S^2 = \frac{(f_1 m_1^2 + f_2 m_2^2 + \cdots + f_k m_k^2) - \dfrac{(f_1 m_1 + f_2 m_2 + \cdots + f_k m_k)^2}{n}}{n - 1}$$

$$= \frac{\Sigma fm^2 - \dfrac{(\Sigma fm)^2}{n}}{n - 1}$$

Example: The $n = 58$ LOS measurements introduced earlier and summarized into a grouped frequency distribution are again used to calculate S^2 using *only* the computational formula. Because $\overline{X}$ is not a whole number, the use of the definitional formula introduces unnecessary computational complexity. The calculations are shown in table 8-13.

Table 8-12. LOS Variance Computation for June Using Definitional and Computational Formulas

X = LOS	$X - \bar{X}$	$(X - \bar{X})^2$	X^2
6	−1	1	36
9	2	4	81
9	2	4	81
6	−1	1	36
5	−2	4	25
7	0	0	49
42	0	14	308

$n = 6$

$\bar{X} = \dfrac{42}{6} = 7.0$

Definitional formula:

$$S^2 = \frac{\Sigma(X - \bar{X})^2}{n - 1} = \frac{14}{5} = 2.80$$

Computational formula:

$$S^2 = \frac{\Sigma X^2 - \dfrac{(\Sigma X)^2}{n}}{n - 1} = \frac{308 - \dfrac{(42)^2}{6}}{5}$$

$$= \frac{14}{5} = 2.80$$

$$S = \sqrt{2.80}$$

$$= 1.67 \text{ days}$$

Table 8-13. LOS Variance Computation from Grouped Frequency Distribution Using the Computational Formula

Class	f	m	fm	fm^2
1	2	2	4	8
2	12	4	48	192
3	17	6	102	612
4	14	8	112	896
5	8	10	80	800
6	3	12	36	432
7	2	14	28	392
	58 = n		410	3,332

$$S^2 = \frac{\Sigma fm^2 - \dfrac{(\Sigma fm)^2}{n}}{n - 1}$$

$$= \frac{3332 - \dfrac{(410)^2}{58}}{57}$$

$$= \frac{433.72}{57}$$

$$= 7.61$$

$$S = \sqrt{7.61}$$

$$= 2.76 \text{ days}$$

Conclusion

The measures of variability introduced here—range, variance, and standard deviation—are all intended to summarize the dispersion of a data set. The variance and standard deviation are the preferred measures for purposes of most statistical analyses, such as those in the forthcoming section on statistical inference. However, the range is useful and will be revisited later in the section on statistical process control.

Measures for Qualitative Data

Measures of central tendency and variability have been discussed in the context of quantitative data. It is also necessary to summarize measurements that are qualitative. *Proportions* and *rates* are the two most commonly used measures when summarizing qualitative data.

Notationally, we define

π (Greek letter pi) = population proportion
= proportion or percentage of units in the population having the attribute or characteristic of interest
P = sample proportion

Because π is generally unavailable, its sample counterpart P will be used, as was done with quantitative summary measures.

Let

n = the number of units of analysis in the sample
y = the number of units of analysis in the sample having the characteristic of interest.

Then

$$P = \frac{y}{n}$$

P can range from 0 to 1 and alternatively be multiplied by 100 percent and expressed as a percentage.

A rate is an alternative way of expressing a percentage or proportion. When P is very small, this is a convenient alternative. A rate is simply a proportion multiplied by some constant (for example, 100, 1,000, 10,000) and expressed as a rate per the chosen constant. Let K = the constant, then

$$\text{rate} = P \times K$$

Example: Consider a scenario where the patients that undergo a surgical procedure at a hospital during a year constitute the units of analysis. The qualitative measurement made on each patient is his or her status at discharge: whether he or she is alive or dead. Suppose

n = 240 patients discharged
y = 3 dead

Hence

$$P = \frac{y}{n}$$

$$= \frac{3}{240} = .0125$$

Expressed as a percentage, 1.25 percent of the patients undergoing the procedure at this hospital died. Equivalently, one could choose $K = 1,000$ as a constant and compute the following:

$$\begin{aligned} \text{rate} &= P \times K \\ &= .0125 \times 1,000 \\ &= 12.5 \text{ deaths per } 1,000 \text{ patients} \end{aligned}$$

This would be the mortality rate per 1,000 patients for individuals undergoing the surgical procedure at this hospital during the chosen year.

This two-category situation can easily be extended to more than two categories. In this case, one would simply compute the percentage of units in each category and convert into rates, if desired.

Example: Suppose 310 patients having a particular disease at the same hospital during the same time period are further stratified into four categories—I, II, III, and IV—reflecting the degree of disease progression (that is, severity of illness) with IV being the most severe.

Category	Number of Patients
I	202
II	89
III	16
IV	3
	310

The proportion in each category and the rate per 100 patients having the disease is given by

Category	Proportion	Rate per 100 Patients
I	202/310 = .6516	65.16
II	89/310 = .2871	28.71
III	16/310 = .0516	5.16
IV	3/310 = .0097	.97
	1.0000	100.00

Proportions and rates are useful measurements when making comparisons involving different numbers of units of analysis. They are essential when summarizing qualitative measurements.

Other Measures

A variety of other measures exist, principally for characterizing other aspects of quantitative data. Two of these measures are worthy of brief description here: *Z-scores* and *percentiles*. Each of these measures are positional; that is, they describe the position that a certain data value occupies in an ordered data set.

Z-Score

In units of standard deviations, a Z-score measures the difference between a data item and the mean of the overall data set. Letting $X = $ an individual data item:

$$\text{population } Z\text{-score} = \frac{X - \mu}{\sigma}$$

$$\text{sample } Z\text{-score} = \frac{X - \overline{X}}{S}$$

In each case the difference between X and the mean is found and then divided into units of standard deviations. In other words Z is the number of standard deviations that X falls away from the mean. If Z is negative, X is *below* the mean; if Z is positive, X is *above* the mean. Thus, Z equaling zero implies that X equals the mean.

Example: Assume that a sample of eight hospitals has the following annual average LOS (in days) for a particular DRG:

Hospital	Average LOS
A	4.5
B	5.1
C	4.7
D	6.2
E	4.9
F	4.6
G	5.2
H	5.3

To find the corresponding Z-scores for each hospital, calculate $\overline{X}$ and S:

$$n = 8$$
$$\Sigma X = 40.5$$
$$\Sigma X^2 = 207.09$$

$$\overline{X} = \frac{\Sigma X}{n} = \frac{40.5}{8} = 5.06 \text{ days}$$

$$S^2 = \frac{\Sigma X^2 - \dfrac{(\Sigma X)^2}{n}}{n - 1} = \frac{207.09 - \dfrac{(40.5)^2}{8}}{7} = .2941$$

$$S = \sqrt{.2941} = .54 \text{ days}$$

So, for hospital A:

$$Z = \frac{X - \overline{X}}{S} = \frac{4.5 - 5.06}{.54} = -1.04$$

This indicates that hospital A is 1.04 standard deviations below the overall average LOS for the hospitals under study. Similarly for hospital D:

$$Z = \frac{X - \overline{X}}{S} = \frac{6.2 - 5.06}{.54} = +2.11$$

This demonstrates that hospital D is 2.11 standard deviations above the group average. For all hospitals:

Hospital	Average LOS	Z-Score
A	4.5	−1.04
B	5.1	.07
C	4.7	−.67
D	6.2	2.11
E	4.9	−.30
F	4.6	−.85
G	5.2	.26
H	5.3	.44

Collectively these hospitals are fairly similar to each other except for hospital D, which has a considerably higher average LOS than the others.

The Z-score is a useful comparison measure in that it uses both the mean and standard deviation, simultaneously reflecting both central tendency and variability.

Percentiles

As with Z-scores, percentiles are positional measures. There are 99 percentiles (P_1, P_2, . . . , P_{99}) for any given data set. Collectively they partition the ordered data into 100 parts. By definition, the kth percentile P_k divides the data set into two parts: $k\%$ below P_k and $(100 − k)\%$ above P_k.

The percentile P_{50} has already been encountered; that is the median of a data set. Other common percentiles include P_{25} and P_{75}, also called the *1st and 3rd quartiles, Q_1 and Q_3,* respectively. P_{50} is also referred to as the *2nd quartile,* or Q_2. As can be deduced, quartiles divide a data set into quarters or fourths.

There will be no discussion in this chapter of procedures for computing percentiles from either individual measurements or grouped frequency distribution data. However, procedures for doing so can be found in a number of textbooks.[13-16] The following section extends the previous discussion of numerical summary measures to methods for making inferences about a population from a sample.

☐ Statistical Inference

In using sample data taken from a population, the fundamental goal is to estimate the numerical value of one or more parameters (that is, μ or π) of the population, or to test some conjecture about the value of the parameter(s). The two basic approaches taken in statistical inference are *estimation* and *hypothesis testing.*

Caveats on Coverage

The field of statistical inference is a broad and multifaceted subject. The choice of analytical approach is guided by various characteristics of the data under study, such as:

- Size of the sample
- Parameter(s) of interest (that is, quantitative or qualitative measurement)
- Type of distribution of the units of analysis for the variable under study in the population from which the sample was taken (that is, whether the distribution is symmetrically bell shaped or has some other form)
- How the sample was selected

The choice is also influenced by the kind of question to be addressed by the analysis. For example, one may wish to simply estimate the mean of a single population or test the equality of the proportions for two populations.

This chapter is concerned with the inspection of data. One logical component of this process is estimation and hypothesis testing. However, as neither scope nor space allows an in-depth treatment, the following limiting assumptions will be made for this discussion:

- *The size of the sample being used for inference is large.* For quantitative data this will be taken to be $n = 30$ or more. For qualitative data $n = 100$ or more will be assumed so that certain conditions on the relationship between n and p will be met.
- *The mean and proportion are the only parameters examined.* Both quantitative and qualitative measurements have been examined, and because the mean (μ) and the proportion (π) are the most commonly used parameters in each situation, the focus will be on these two only.
- *A normal (mound- or bell-shaped) distribution is used for purposes of inference.* By virtue of the sample sizes presumed for study, it has been demonstrated that the normal distribution is appropriate to use when making statistical inferences about μ and π. However, if one were to have a small sample size and/or be interested in other parameters, such as σ^2, the normal distribution assumption would not be appropriate.
- *The sample is assumed to be selected via simple random sampling.* Concepts of sampling were covered in chapter 1. The inferential techniques to be described here require that the data represent a simple random sample selected from the population under study.

If the reader needs more in-depth coverage of statistical inference, the references at the end of this chapter should be consulted. The purpose of the following discussion is simply to incorporate statistical inference as a logical component of the inspection of data.

Estimation

For purposes of this discussion, the value of an unknown parameter from a population is to be approximated using the data from a sample. There are two kinds of estimates:

- *Point estimate:* a single numerical value computed from the sample, taken to best represent the population parameter
- *Interval estimate:* a range of values for the parameter, computed from the sample, in which one has a certain stated confidence that the parameter falls

Point Estimates

Statistical theory states that the best point estimates for estimating the mean and proportion of a population from sample data are as follows:

Parameter	Point estimate
μ = population mean	$\overline{X}$ = sample mean
π = population proportion	P = sample proportion

The computations surrounding $\overline{X}$ and P from quantitative and qualitative data, respectively, were presented in the previous section on summary measures. The use of the *sample statistic* (that is, point estimate) corresponding to the population parameter is logical. Using various criteria in statistical theory, it is also well established that these are the optimal estimates.

Interval Estimates

An interval estimate, or *confidence interval*, is an extremely useful way of modifying a point estimate to take into account *sampling error*. Sampling error is the unavoidable potential error that results from using a sample instead of a population. Basically, most interval estimates have the following generic format:

point estimate ± potential sampling error

The actual derivation of formulas for interval estimates involves the use of probability theory and more mathematics than will be attempted here; however, the basic procedure for constructing a confidence interval from sample data will be presented, followed by the interpretation and use of such estimates in the health care environment. Interval estimates for both μ and π are given.

Mean

The goal is to find two numbers *a* and *b* in order to state

$$a \leq \mu \leq b$$

with a certain degree of confidence, say 95 percent or 99 percent. The actual numerical values for *a* and *b* are determined using the sample data, namely,

n = sample size
$\overline{X}$ = sample mean
S = sample standard deviation

Also, before actually computing *a* and *b*, one must specify the desired *probability* that the interval will include the unknown parameter μ. This could be .90, .95, or .99, for example. It should be noted that selecting 1.00 is unreasonable, because a sample cannot achieve perfect estimation. After actually calculating the numerical values for *a* and *b* from the data, probability becomes *confidence*, because the interval so computed is only one realization of a process. This process has generated one interval that either does or does not contain the unknown μ. Hence we use the term *confidence interval*.

To find the values for *a* and *b*, it is necessary to refer to the previously stated caveats and apply the concept of a bell-shaped relative frequency distribution, called the *normal probability distribution*, to describe how $\overline{X}$ varies from sample to sample. Simply stated, as more confidence is desired, the normal distribution will generate wider confidence limits on μ, through a factor Z included in the computation of the limits. For ease of use, and to avoid the necessity of having a table of the standard normal distribution, the following widely used constants are provided:

Confidence Desired	Normal Distribution Z-Value
90%	1.645
95%	1.960
99%	2.575

As can be seen, more confidence yields larger Z-values and, as will be seen, wider (more conservative) limits on μ.

The formulas for *a* and *b* combine the sample data (n, $\overline{X}$, and S) with the Z-value and are as follows:

$$a = \overline{X} - Z\frac{S}{\sqrt{n}}$$

$$b = \overline{X} + Z\frac{S}{\sqrt{n}}$$

The limits *a* and *b* are symmetrical about $\overline{X}$; that is, they are each an equal distance above and below $\overline{X}$, respectively. As can be seen, the width of the interval is affected in the following ways:

Change in Conditions	Impact on Interval Width
Higher confidence level	Wider interval
Larger standard deviation	Wider interval
Larger sample size	Narrower interval

Example: Suppose one is interested in determining the average diastolic blood pressure (μ) on admission for all the patients treated by a hospital during a particular year. This information is available because it is kept in each patient's chart. However, in this case, assume it is not computerized. Further, suppose this estimate of μ is needed quite soon so that it becomes necessary to use sampling.

A simple random sample of 200 patient charts is selected for review. The diastolic blood pressure (X) for each patient is extracted and recorded. From these data the following summary statistics are obtained:

$$n = 200$$
$$\overline{X} = 78.69$$
$$S = 10.49$$

It is decided that 95 percent confidence will be used to obtain a confidence interval for μ, so $Z = 1.96$. Hence,

$$a = \overline{X} - Z\frac{S}{\sqrt{n}}$$

$$= 78.69 - 1.96\frac{10.49}{\sqrt{200}}$$

$$= 78.69 - 1.45 = 77.24$$

$$b = \overline{X} + Z\frac{S}{\sqrt{n}}$$

$$= 78.69 + 1.45 = 80.14$$

Thus, with 95 percent confidence it can be stated that for *all* patients from which this sample was taken the average diastolic blood pressure has the following limits:

$$77.24 \le \mu \le 80.14$$

Now suppose someone suggests that a 99 percent confidence level is more appropriate. Here, $Z = 2.575$ and the calculations are repeated.

$$a, b = \overline{X} \pm Z\frac{S}{\sqrt{n}}$$

$$= 78.69 \pm 2.575\frac{10.49}{\sqrt{200}}$$

$$= 78.69 \pm 1.91$$

Thus, with 99 percent confidence

$$76.78 \leq \mu \leq 80.60$$

Using a sample of only 200 patients, one is able to find a confidence interval for the average diastolic blood pressure that is not only quite accurate in estimating μ, but also with a high level of confidence.

Proportion

The objective now is to find two numbers c and d such that

$$c \leq \pi \leq d$$

with a specified level of confidence. As before, c and d will be obtained from sample data:

n = sample size
P = sample proportion having the characteristic of interest

The Z-value associated with the chosen level of confidence will again be used. The formulas for c and d follow:

$$c = P - Z\sqrt{\frac{P(1 - P)}{n}}$$

$$d = P + Z\sqrt{\frac{P(1 - P)}{n}}$$

The interpretation of these limits is exactly as with the interval for μ, except that the parameter under estimation is the proportion (for qualitative data) as opposed to the mean (for quantitative data).

Example: The results of the interval estimation for average diastolic blood pressure led to a further request to examine a qualitative characteristic: whether or not a patient had a family history of heart disease. In response, the same previously sampled 200 patients had their records examined again. The results were:

$$n = 200$$
$$P = .286$$

That is, 28.6 percent of the sample had a family history of heart disease. A 95 percent confidence interval was found first using $Z = 1.96$:

$$c = .286 - 1.96\sqrt{\frac{.286(1 - .286)}{200}}$$

$$= .286 - .063 = .223$$

$$d = .286 + .063 = .349$$

So, the 95 percent interval estimate for π (the population proportion of all patients having a family history of heart disease) for all patients from which this sample was taken, is given by

$$.223 \leq \pi \leq .349$$

If a 99 percent confidence interval were preferred, $Z = 2.575$ would be substituted. The result would be

$$.204 \leq \pi \leq .368$$

As expected, the 99 percent confidence interval is slightly wider than that for 95 percent confidence.

Conclusion

Using data already available in the sample, one can easily improve on the point estimate, using a confidence interval. The concepts of confidence and sample size, as well as other information from the sample, permit a better estimation of the value of an unknown population parameter for either quantitative or qualitative measurements.

Hypothesis Testing

As stated before, the fundamental goal of statistical inference is to estimate the value of a parameter or to test some conjecture about the value of the parameter. Hypothesis tests can be performed for parameters of distributions for either quantitative or qualitative measurements.

Basically, two possible conjectures are made about the value of a parameter, the so-called null and alternative hypotheses. For example, in the previous case of diastolic blood pressure estimation one might have decided instead to test a statistical hypothesis of the form:

Null hypothesis: $\mu \geq 80$
Alternative hypothesis: $\mu < 80$

This could arise from a desire to compare data on the patients in this hospital with national data on diastolic blood pressure. If one wanted to show that the patients in this hospital had a *lower* average diastolic blood pressure, the above hypotheses would be tested using data from a sample selected from the hospital under study. Based on these data and the laws of probability, one of two courses of action would be determined:

- Reject the null hypothesis in favor of the alternative hypothesis.
- Do no reject (that is, accept) the null hypothesis.

A similar hypothesis-testing scenario could be constructed in the example where π = population proportion of patients having a family history of heart disease. If the national proportion were really 25 percent, one might want to see whether the sample indicates that the patient population has a *higher* prevalence of this characteristic than nationally. To test this, one would use:

Null hypothesis: $\pi \leq .25$
Alternative hypothesis: $\pi > .25$

For tests involving either μ or π, one would then follow a procedure whereby the sample data would be used to decide whether to reject the null hypothesis. Of course, because only sample data are involved, one could be wrong in either of two ways:

- A true null hypothesis could be rejected.
- A false null hypothesis could be accepted.

The statistical theory underlying hypothesis testing is designed to minimize such errors. Furthermore, the decision maker has some flexibility in selecting the level of protection against these errors.

Statistical tests were examined in greater depth in chapter 3 of this book. A number of texts are available that deal extensively with statistical tests.[17-20]

☐ Exploratory Data Analysis

This chapter would be sorely incomplete if the techniques of exploratory data analysis (EDA) were not introduced. These methods were first proposed in the early 1970s by John W. Tukey and since that time have been widely used and applied in a variety of problem settings.

Collectively, the techniques are useful in a number of situations. Velleman and Hoaglin suggest that "four major ingredients of EDA stand out:

- *Displays* visually reveal the behavior of the data and the structure of the analyses;
- *Residuals* focus attention on what remains of the data after some analysis;
- *Reexpressions,* by means of simple mathematical functions such as the logarithm and the square root, help to simplify behavior and clarify analyses; and
- *Resistance* ensures that a few extraordinary data values do not unduly influence the results of an analysis."[21]

In the brief treatment of EDA that follows, only displays are discussed. The inspection and analysis of health care quality data could certainly benefit from applications of the latter three ingredients, as well. The reader is therefore encouraged to consult additional references on EDA, should the need or interest arise.[22,23]

The advantages of such graphic displays as histograms in the examination of a single set of quantitative data were pointed out previously in this chapter. Two methods of EDA are also useful for this purpose: *stem-and-leaf displays* and *box plots.* Despite the fact that these techniques are conceptually simple, they are very instructive in the inspection of data.

Stem-and-Leaf Displays

For this statistical graphic it is assumed that the data are not classified in any particular way and that their organization is of interest. Consequently, the first step is to sort the data into (usually ascending) numerical order. The digits themselves are allowed to provide the graphic display. A preselected number of digits is used at the beginning of each data value as a categorization and basis for sorting. These are called *leading digits,* or *stems.* The next digits, called *trailing digits,* or *leaves,* then form the display. The following example should clarify the procedure.

Example: Data showing the surgical mortality rate per 100 patients for coronary artery bypass grafts (CABG) at 30 critical care hospitals are provided in table 8-14. Figure 8-7 presents those same data in a stem-and-leaf display. Note that the first two digits' values range from 40 to 55, for a total of 16 classes. For illustration, then, the data values can be split so that the leading digits or stems are the values 40 to 55. These digits are then written down sequentially in a column, including leading digits that might not have actually occurred in the data. Next a vertical line is drawn after these stems. This line divides the stems from the leaves. To the right of the line, the trailing digit or leaf is listed for each data value having that stem.

Table 8-14. Surgical Mortality Rate for CABG at 30 Critical Care Hospitals

Hospital	Rate	Hospital	Rate
1	4.71	16	5.04
2	5.22	17	4.31
3	4.58	18	4.95
4	4.55	19	4.05
5	4.65	20	5.38
6	5.19	21	4.83
7	4.46	22	4.61
8	5.07	23	4.59
9	4.17	24	4.98
10	4.82	25	4.25
11	4.47	26	4.53
12	4.64	27	4.76
13	5.52	28	4.49
14	4.50	29	4.67
15	4.33	30	5.16

Figure 8-7. Stem-and-Leaf Display of the Data in Table 8-14

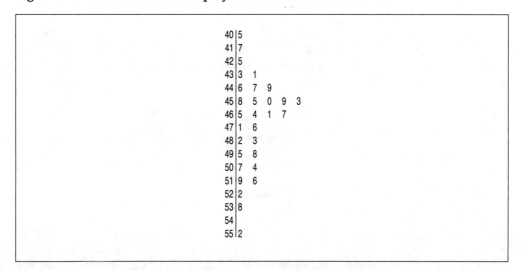

```
40|5
41|7
42|5
43|3 1
44|6 7 9
45|8 5 0 9 3
46|5 4 1 7
47|1 6
48|2 3
49|5 8
50|7 4
51|9 6
52|2
53|8
54|
55|2
```

The display in figure 8-7 allows for easy visual interpretation of the data's distribution, in the same fashion as a histogram. Although constructing stem-and-leaf displays can be somewhat tedious, personal computer (PC) and mainframe computer statistical packages are well adapted to produce them.

Example: Data in table 8-15 show that 43 patients underwent cardiovascular surgery at a certain hospital during a given period of time. The data in that table can be arranged in a stem-and-leaf display to examine patient ages, as shown in figure 8-8. Figure 8-8 was produced using a widely available PC statistical package.

In figure 8-8, two "LO" outliers are identified: 35 and 42. The rest of the display shows stems with either * or ○. A * represents leaf second digits 0 through 4, and ○ represents second digits 5 through 9. For example, 5*|1 represents individual 32 whose age is 51 and 7○|5 is individual 36 whose age is 75. The computer program makes a number of simplifying assumptions that greatly reduce the effort involved in the construction of a stem-and-leaf display.

Table 8-15. Ages of 43 Cardiovascular Surgery Patients

Patient	Age	Patient	Age
1	64	23	67
2	73	24	63
3	68	25	77
4	63	26	73
5	74	27	58
6	64	28	57
7	70	29	61
8	59	30	66
9	73	31	88
10	66	32	51
11	55	33	72
12	68	34	77
13	42	35	76
14	59	36	75
15	70	37	69
16	74	38	62
17	63	39	59
18	76	40	62
19	62	41	66
20	72	42	35
21	57	43	74
22	80		

Figure 8-8. Stem-and-Leaf Display of the Data in Table 8-15

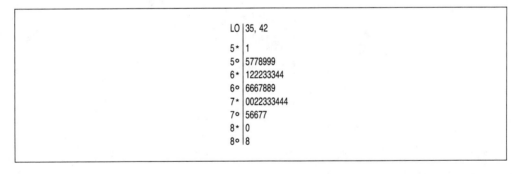

```
LO | 35, 42

 5* | 1
 5° | 5778999
 6* | 122233344
 6° | 6667889
 7* | 0022333444
 7° | 56677
 8* | 0
 8° | 8
```

A variety of details concerning stem-and-leaf displays have been omitted here. For example, the * and ° partitioning of stems into two groups can be extended to multiple lines per stem, and a number of other variants exist, as well.

Box Plots

The box plot is another statistical graphic for presenting a single set of quantitative data. However, it is an even simpler and more compact way of summarizing a data set than a stem-and-leaf display. Its basic objective is to provide a picture of where the middle of the data set is, how dispersed the data are, and how the tails (or extremes) relate to the data set.

To illustrate the concept of a box plot, the construction of a *skeletal box plot*, the simplest form of box plot, is described. In essence, a skeletal box plot is a five-number summary of a data set. It uses the median, two *hinges,* and two extremes. The extremes are the minimum and maximum values in the data set. The hinges are similar to the first and third quartiles, Q_1 and Q_3, discussed earlier. The hinges differ from Q_1 and Q_3 in that they are compiled relative to the median; that is, the lower hinge is the median of the lower half of the data set, and the upper hinge is the median of the upper half. Figure 8-9 is a box plot for the hospital surgical mortality rate data presented in table 8-14.

The median is located at the vertical line inside the horizontal box and indicates the middle of the data set. The left and right extremes of the box are the lower and upper hinges, respectively. The extensions to the left and right, often called *whiskers*, extend to the minimum and maximum, respectively. The distance between the lower and upper hinges shows the range over which roughly the middle half of the data extends. The two whiskers give an indication of the magnitude of the extreme values. Here, the skew is to the right, that is, toward larger mortality rates, as would be expected in this situation.

Figure 8-10 is a box plot showing the patient age data from table 8-15. As can be seen, this distribution is somewhat more compact but does have two lower-end outliers (the ages 35 and 42 seen previously), indicated by the two small squares at the left of the figure. Figures 8-9 and 8-10 were both produced using a widely available PC statistical package.

The box plot is a versatile and easy tool to use. Because this discussion can only serve as a basic introduction, further reading is encouraged.

Conclusion

The stem-and-leaf display and the box plot are only two of a variety of EDA techniques. Their broad use in the inspection of data from the health care delivery environment is strongly indicated because of the four "ingredients" pointed out at the beginning of this discussion.

In the next and final part of this chapter, statistical methods for process control and improvement are introduced.

☐ Statistical Process Control

Statistical process control (SPC) has long been used with considerable success for process control and improvement in traditional industrial and manufacturing settings. Only in the past few years have these industrial methods begun to capture the interest and imagination of health care practitioners and decision makers. As with EDA, only a brief introduction to a few of the ideas of SPC will be provided here. A number of texts are on the market that offer in-depth discussion of this subject.[24-28]

Collectively, SPC methods are concerned with the use of measurements to study a process with the goal of making it perform in a certain way, conform to standards, and continuously improve. The use of SPC methods builds on the previous discussion of data collection, presentation, and analysis. This introduction focuses on only one facet of SPC, the use of control charts for the display and analysis of data. Three types of control charts—$\overline{X}$, R, and P—are examined. The $\overline{X}$ and R charts are used with quantitative data; the P charts are applied to qualitative data. These graphics allow the inspection of data about a process that, when examined statistically, can be used to learn about that process and, in turn, help to improve it.

$\overline{X}$ and R Charts

When examining quantitative measurements such as length of stay (LOS), two aspects of the measurements are of primary interest:

- Central tendency
- Variability

Figure 8-9. Box Plot of Hospital Surgical Mortality Rate Data from Table 8-14

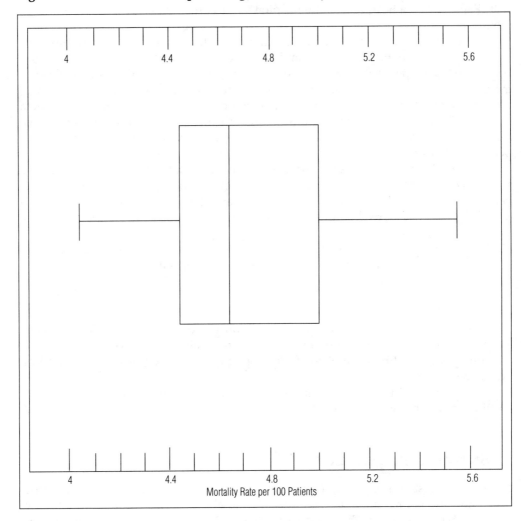

Mortality Rate per 100 Patients

These aspects of quantitative data were examined in the previous discussion of summary measures. $\overline{X}$ and R charts, respectively, allow one to examine and monitor both central tendency and variability. This monitoring can use a time period (for example, a month), a department, a hospital, or some other reasonable collection as the *element* over which units of analysis are *aggregated*.

To illustrate the construction of $\overline{X}$ and R charts, the monthly LOS data introduced previously in table 8-4 will be used. For these data, the monthly number of patients, the mean LOS, and the range of LOS were obtained for each month and are shown in table 8-16.

$\overline{X}$ Charts

An $\overline{X}$ chart is used to examine differences between elements of aggregation with respect to the average measurement for each. Basically, a control chart for $\overline{X}$ involves plotting each element's mean, then constructing upper and lower "control limits," and finally identifying those elements outside the limits, that is, those elements that are "out of control." Figure 8-11 shows the generic format of an $\overline{X}$ chart.

Figure 8-10. Box Plot of Cardiovascular Surgery Patient Age Data from Table 8-15

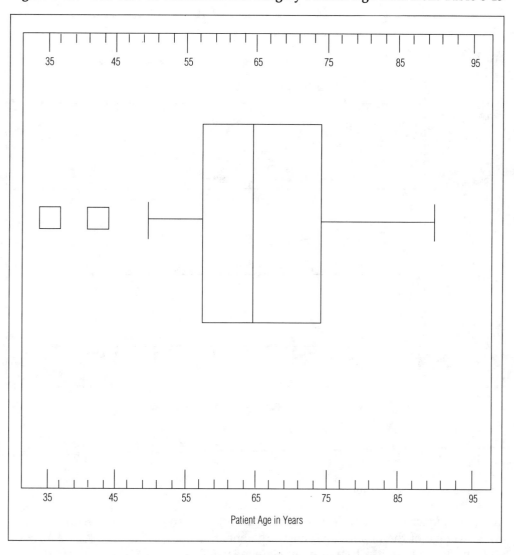

Patient Age in Years

Table 8-16. Summary Statistics for Monthly LOS for Patients in DRG XXX for Hospital Y, during 19ZZ

Month	i	Number of Patients (n_i)	Average ($\bar{X}_i$)	Range (R_i)
Jan.	1	4	7.50	10
Feb.	2	4	7.00	8
Mar.	3	4	8.00	3
Apr.	4	6	7.33	8
May	5	2	4.00	4
June	6	6	7.00	4
July	7	7	6.57	9
Aug.	8	7	7.57	11
Sept.	9	6	6.00	6
Oct.	10	2	6.50	1
Nov.	11	5	6.00	5
Dec.	12	5	4.60	5

Figure 8-11. Generic Format of an $\overline{X}$ Control Chart

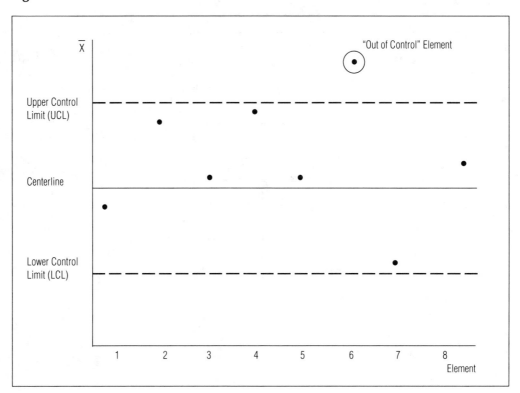

Notationally, let

i = index for the elements used for aggregation = 1, 2, . . . , k
k = number of elements to be control charted
n_i = sample size for element i = number of units of analysis in element i
$\overline{X}_i$ = average of the quantitative measurements
        from the n_i units of analysis in element i
R_i = range of the quantitative measurements from the n_i units of analysis in element i

Next, the centerline, the upper control limit (UCL) and the lower control limit (LCL) need to be found. For the centerline the grand mean of all the measurements is used:

$$\text{centerline} = \overline{\overline{X}} = \frac{1}{n}\Sigma n_i \overline{X}_i$$

where

$$n = \Sigma n_i$$

Here $\overline{\overline{X}}$ is the weighted (by n_i) average of each individual element's mean ($\overline{X}_i$). Hence, for the data in table 8-16:

$$n = \Sigma n_i$$
$$= 4 + 4 + \cdots + 5 = 58$$

and

$$\bar{\bar{X}} = \frac{1}{n}\Sigma n_i \bar{X}_i$$

$$= \frac{1}{58}[4(7.50) + 4(7.00) + \cdots + 5(4.60)]$$

$$= 6.64$$

$\bar{\bar{X}}$ could also be obtained by averaging the 58 original LOS values (table 8-4).

To find the UCL and LCL, the "process sigma," which measures the overall process variability, must now be found. An approximation of this quantity is found from the ranges. Let

$$\bar{R} = \frac{1}{k}\Sigma R_i = \text{average range}$$

$$\bar{n} = \frac{1}{k}\Sigma n_i = \text{average sample size}$$

$$\text{sigma} = \frac{\bar{R}}{d_2} = \sigma$$

where d_2 = a constant from table 8-17, chosen according to the value of $\bar{n}$.

Here,

$$\bar{R} = \frac{1}{12}[10 + 8 + \cdots + 5]$$

$$= \frac{1}{12}(74) = 6.16667$$

$$\bar{n} = \frac{1}{12}(4 + 4 + \cdots + 5)$$

$$= \frac{1}{12}(58) = 4.8333$$

For $\bar{n} = 4.8333$, interpolate between the d_2 entries for $n = 4$ and $n = 5$ in table 8-17. This gives

$$d_2 = 2.059 + (4.8333 - 4) \times (2.326 - 2.059)$$
$$= 2.281$$

So

$$\sigma = \frac{6.16667}{2.281}$$

$$= 2.70349$$

$$= 2.703$$

Table 8-17. Factors for Control Limit Computation

n	d_2	d_3
2	1.128	0.853
3	1.693	0.888
4	2.059	0.880
5	2.326	0.864
6	2.534	0.848
7	2.704	0.833
8	2.847	0.820
9	2.970	0.808
10	3.078	0.797
11	3.173	0.787
12	3.258	0.778
13	3.336	0.770
14	3.407	0.762
15	3.472	0.755
16	3.532	0.749
17	3.588	0.743
18	3.640	0.738
19	3.689	0.733
20	3.735	0.729
21	3.778	0.724
22	3.819	0.720
23	3.858	0.716
24	3.895	0.712
25	3.931	0.709

Source: Copyright ASTM. Reprinted with permission.

Finally,

$$\text{UCL, LCL} = \overline{\overline{X}} \pm C\frac{\sigma}{\sqrt{n}}$$

where C is a constant chosen by the analyst.

If $C = 2$, these are so-called 2 sigma limits. Two sigma limits are expected to include roughly 95 percent of the $\overline{X}$s for the elements under study, if the process that generates them is "in control." If $C = 3$, over 99 percent of the $\overline{X}$s should be contained in the limits, if the process is "in control." However, one must make the assumption that the $\overline{X}$s are normally distributed to use the percentage interpretation (that is, 95 percent, 99 percent).

Here, $C = 2$ will be used:

$$\text{UCL, LCL} = 6.64 \pm 2\frac{2.703}{\sqrt{4.8333}}$$

$$= 6.64 \pm 2.46$$

$$= 4.18, 9.10$$

Figure 8-12 shows the final $\overline{X}$ chart with monthly average lengths of stay indexed on the vertical axis and month on the horizontal axis. The UCL, LCL, and centerline (computed to more decimal places of accuracy by a PC) are as previously calculated.

From figure 8-12, it can be seen that month 5 has a LOS that is below the LCL and merits review. Though excessively long LOSs consume valuable resources, extremely short LOS values could indicate possible problems as well.

Figure 8-12. $\bar{X}$ **Chart for Monthly LOS Data from Table 8-16**

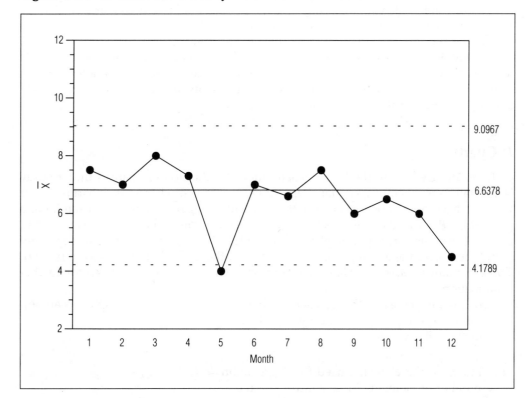

R Charts

An R chart is used to examine variability by obtaining and graphing the range in measurements for each element. Its construction is similar to that of an $\bar{X}$ chart in that it has a centerline, UCL, and LCL. It is obtained as follows:

$$\text{centerline} = \bar{R}$$

$$\text{UCL, LCL} = \bar{R}\left(1 \pm C\frac{d_3}{d_2}\right)$$

where d_2 and d_3 are found in table 8-17. It is likely that interpolation between entries for noninteger values of $\bar{n}$ will be necessary for both d_2 and d_3. C is as described before.

For the data in table 8-16, it was previously found that

$$\text{centerline} = \bar{R} = 6.16667$$

From table 8-17 with $\bar{n} = 4.8333$

$$d_2 = 2.281 \text{ (from before)}$$
$$d_3 = .880 + (4.8333 - 4) \times (.864 - .880)$$
$$= .867$$

So, using $C = 2$ as before

$$\text{UCL, LCL} = 6.16667\left(1 \pm 2\frac{.867}{2.281}\right)$$

$$= 1.48, 10.85$$

Figure 8-13 shows the control chart constructed for individual monthly ranges obtained from table 8-16, with the centerline, UCL, and LCL. From this chart considerable month-to-month variation can be seen. In fact, months 8 and 10 are above the UCL and below the LCL, respectively. Clearly this variability merits further exploration.

Finally, it has become a common practice in control charting using $\bar{X}$ and R charts to show them on the same page. In this way, the analyst can explore adherence to central location and examine variation within elements simultaneously. Figure 8-14 is a presentation of the previous $\bar{X}$ and R charts.

P Charts

P charts are used when the basic measurement for the unit of analysis under study is qualitative, for example, a patient being alive or dead at discharge. A P chart is similar to an $\bar{X}$ chart in its basic format. For the elements of aggregation being examined, a proportion P is calculated for each element. Based on these data, a centerline, UCL, and LCL are calculated and displayed on a graph. Letting the vertical axis represent P and the horizontal axis represent the elements, the individual P values are plotted. Those P values above the UCL or below the LCL are then candidates for further examination.

To illustrate, consider the data set in table 8-18 on mortality by hospital as an outcome of a surgical procedure during a particular period.

Notationally, we define

i = index for the elements used for aggregation = 1, 2, . . . , k
k = number of elements to be control charted
n_i = sample size for element i = number of units of analysis in element i
y_i = number of units of analysis in element i having the characteristic of interest
P_i = proportion of units of analysis in element i having the characteristic of interest
    = y_i/n_i

Then

$$\bar{P} = \text{centerline} = \frac{\Sigma y_i}{\Sigma n_i}$$

$$= \frac{44}{2547}$$

$$= .01728$$

An alternative way of finding the centerline is using the n_i and P_i:

$$\bar{P} = \frac{\Sigma n_i P_i}{\Sigma n_i}$$

$$= \frac{37(.000) + 60(.033) + \cdots + 543(.022)}{2547}$$

$$= .01724$$

This latter method is slightly less accurate due to roundoff in the P_i. Consequently, the result differs somewhat from the former method.

Figure 8-13. *R* Chart for Monthly LOS Data from Table 8-16

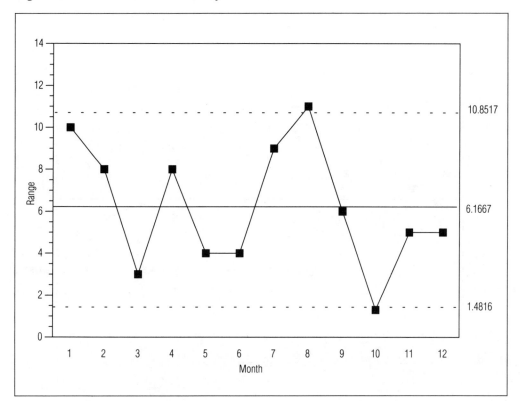

Next, the control limits are given by:

$$\bar{P} \pm C\sqrt{\frac{\bar{P}(1 - \bar{P})}{\bar{n}}}$$

where C and $\bar{n}$ are defined as with $\bar{X}$ and R charts. Here, then

$$\bar{P} = .01728$$

$$\bar{n} = \frac{2547}{15}$$

$$= 169.8$$

Let $C = 2$ (implying 95 percent control limits) so that LCL and UCL are computed as follows:

$$.01728 \pm 2\sqrt{\frac{(.01728)(1 - .01728)}{169.8}} = -.00272, .03728$$

Clearly a negative LCL is inappropriate, and so negative limits are set to zero.

The resultant control chart is given in figure 8-15. Notice that $\bar{P}$ is calculated from the P_i by the statistical package, and so results differ slightly. As can be seen, hospital 5 has a mortality proportion greater than the UCL, thereby suggesting the need for further review. All the rest seem to be "in control."

Figure 8-14. $\bar{X}$ **and** R **Charts for Monthly LOS Data from Table 8-16**

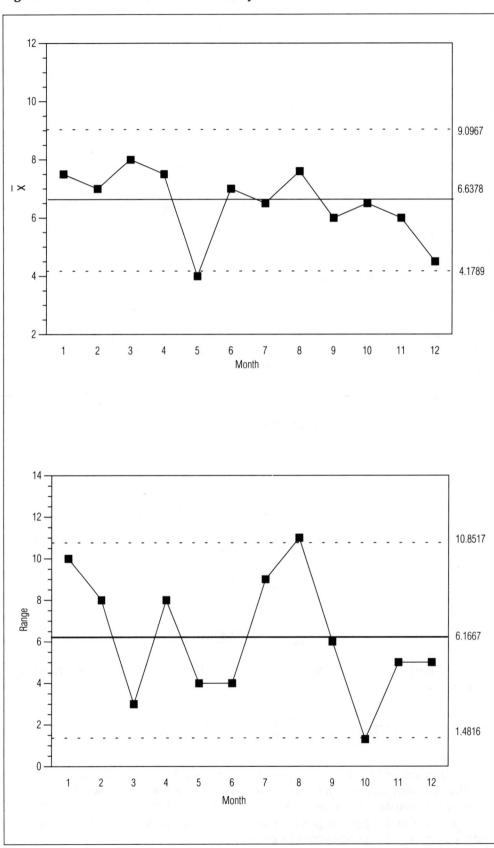

Table 8-18. Mortality Proportion by Hospital for Surgical Procedure ABC

Hospital	i	Number of Patients (n_i)	Number of Deaths (y_i)	Mortality Proportion ($P_i = y_i/n_i$)
A	1	37	0	.000
B	2	60	2	.033
C	3	77	2	.026
D	4	36	1	.028
E	5	45	2	.044
F	6	79	1	.013
G	7	65	1	.015
H	8	120	1	.008
I	9	188	5	.027
J	10	129	3	.023
K	11	178	1	.006
L	12	248	3	.012
M	13	294	4	.014
N	14	448	6	.013
O	15	543	12	.022
		2,547	44	

A strong cautionary note is in order. The interpretation of outlier elements when the n_i differs is difficult using the methods given in this discussion. The UCL and LCL for the $\overline{X}$, R, and P charts, as shown previously, are based on $\overline{n}$ = average sample size. In traditional control charting, the n_i are often equal, or nearly so, implying $\overline{n} \approx n_i$. When this is *not* the case, individual $\overline{X}_i$, R_i, or P_i may be based on a considerably different number of units of analysis (sample size) relative to other elements. Under these circumstances, it is generally wise to calculate individual limits for those elements for which the n_i are quite dissimilar. Details on this are beyond the scope of this chapter but are available in the references.

Although only $\overline{X}$, R, and P charts have been discussed, these are indicative of the usefulness of statistical process control methods, which are currently beginning to be used in health care quality assessment and improvement activities.

☐ Summary

A number of methods for data inspection have been presented in this chapter. These have included basic processing techniques, tabular and graphic displays, summary measures, and some analytical methods—inferential, EDA, and SPC. Each is a fundamental and useful component in the examination of both qualitative and quantitative data. The objective nature of data collection, presentation, and analysis make these tools essential for quality assessment and improvement in the health care environment.

Figure 8-15. *P* **Chart for Mortality Proportion Data from Table 8-18**

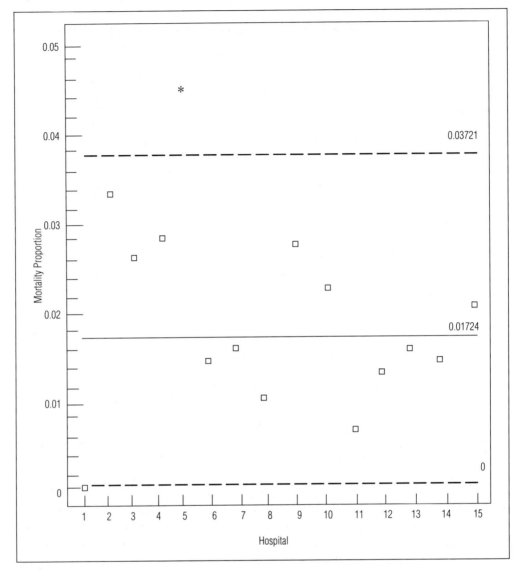

References

1. Sturges, H. A. The choice of a class interval. *Journal of the American Statistical Association* 21:65–66, Mar. 1926.

2. Shiffler, R. E., and Adams, A. J. *Introductory Business Statistics with Microcomputer Applications.* Boston: PWS-Kent Publishing Co., 1990.

3. Chambers, J. M., Cleveland, W. S., Kleiner, B., and Tukey, P. A. *Graphical Methods for Data Analysis.* Pacific Grove, CA: Wadsworth & Brooks/Cole Publishing Co., 1983.

4. Cleveland, W. S. *The Elements of Graphing Data.* Monterey, CA: Wadsworth Advanced Books and Software, 1985.

5. Tufte, E. R. *The Visual Display of Quantitative Information.* Cheshire, CT: Graphics Press, 1983.

6. Huff, D. *How to Lie with Statistics.* New York City: W. W. Norton & Co., 1954.

7. Jaffe, A. J., and Spirer, H. F. *Misused Statistics: Straight Talk for Twisted Numbers.* New York City: Marcel Dekker, 1987.

8. Wainer, H. How to display data badly. *The American Statistician* 38(2):137–47, May 1984.

9. Johnson, R. R. *Elementary Statistics.* 5th ed. Boston: Duxbury Press, 1988.

10. Neter, J., Wasserman, W., and Whitmore, G. A. *Applied Statistics.* 2nd ed. Boston: Allyn and Bacon, 1982.

11. Ostle, B., and Malone, L. C. *Statistics in Research.* 4th ed. Ames, IA: Iowa State University Press, 1988.

12. Shiffler and Adams.

13. Johnson.

14. Neter and others.

15. Ostle and Malone.

16. Shiffler and Adams.

17. Freund, J. E. *Modern Elementary Statistics.* 7th ed. Englewood Cliffs, NJ: Prentice-Hall, 1988.

18. Johnson.

19. Neter and others.

20. Ostle and Malone.

21. Velleman, P. F., and Hoaglin, D. C. *Applications, Basics and Computing of Exploratory Data Analysis.* Boston: Duxbury Press, 1981.

22. McNeil, D. R. *Interactive Data Analysis: A Practical Primer.* New York City: John Wiley and Sons, 1977.

23. Tukey, J. W. *Exploratory Data Analysis.* Reading, MA: Addison-Wesley, 1977.

24. Duncan, A. J. *Quality Control and Industrial Statistics.* 5th ed. Homewood, IL: Richard D. Irwin, 1986.

25. Grant, E. L., and Leavenworth, R. S. *Statistical Quality Control.* 6th ed. New York City: McGraw-Hill Book Co., 1988.

26. Juran, J. M., Gryna, F. M., Jr., and Bingham, R. S., editors. *Quality Control Handbook.* 4th ed. New York City: McGraw-Hill Book Co., 1988.

27. Montgomery, D. C. *An Introduction to Statistical Quality Control.* New York City: John Wiley & Sons, 1985.

28. Western Electric Co. *Statistical Quality Control Handbook.* Indianapolis: AT&T Technologies, 1956.

Section Five

Transforming Data into Information

This section describes the process for making data useful in a real-world context. In this section, the principles of transforming data into information are applied to a study of 289,195 Medicare patients with acute myocardial infarction. The purpose of this section is to provide the reader with the tools needed to develop (1) a more comfortable and useful perspective on data, (2) a clearer understanding of the process that turns data into information, and (3) a template for this process that the reader can then apply to the transformation of his or her own data.

Chapter Nine

Transforming Data into Information:
A Case Study

Richard J. Bogue, Ph.D.

This chapter uses an example from actual practice to provide readers with a common-language framework that will help facilitate their understanding of how data are transformed into information. The example derives from a study of acute myocardial infarctions (AMIs) in Medicare patients. The discussion of the study's background is followed by a description of the data used and generated by the study. The chapter concludes by suggesting a step-by-step process based on the AMI study that will guide readers in their efforts to use their data advantageously.

☐ The AMI Study

In 1989, a study of risk-adjusted, 30-day mortality for patients with fresh acute myocardial infarctions was conducted by Mark S. Blumberg, M.D., Kaiser Foundation Health Plan, Inc., and Gregory S. Binns, Ph.D., Lexecon Health Services, Inc. The study was funded by the AHA Hospital Research and Educational Trust's Quality Measurement and Management Project (QMMP), which is currently sponsored by 15 hospital systems and alliances and whose overall goal is to develop quality monitoring and management tools of choice for hospitals. (The trust is part of the American Hospital Association.)

Among the study's objectives was the preparation of reports for individual hospitals and groups of hospitals and the determination of the usefulness of the reports' formats and contents. The study had other objectives, including assessing the utility of the Quality of Care Medicare Provider Analysis and Review (QC/MedPAR) data set and testing and improving on an indirectly standardized model of risk adjustment. However, the specific focus of this chapter is the process of transforming the data that came out of the study into information for individual hospitals.

Data Collection

To have a clear idea of how the data were defined and intended to be used, it is necessary to understand how they evolved from their raw state to the state in which they were received by the users as final data or results. The raw data for the AMI study were obtained from the 1986–1987 calendar year QC/MedPAR data files from the Health Care Financing Administration (HCFA), which contain Medicare billing data (that is, UB-82). Hospitals submit Medicare billing to fiscal intermediaries for editing, and the information is then consolidated by HCFA.

These data include an encrypted health insurance claim (HIC) number that enables individual patients to be tracked through multiple hospitalizations. The date of death is appended from the Social Security Administration files. In addition, demographic, administrative, and *ICD-9-CM* diagnoses and procedures are included by patient and hospitalization.

For the AMI study the data were further specified. The first criterion for the inclusion of raw data in the study was AMI patients discharged as Medicare cases in 1987. The second set of criteria for limiting the universe of raw data focused on fresh AMI among the Medicare elderly. That is, the researchers took steps to avoid data from disabled Medicare beneficiaries because their risks may have been different from those of the Medicare elderly. The researchers also took steps to avoid data from patients who had suffered an AMI in the eight weeks prior to the AMI in the study because the later admission for AMI might not have represented an accurate episode. The reason for this is that any admission for cardiac problems (for example, angina) that happens within eight weeks of an actual AMI can be coded in HCFA data as an AMI.

These steps involved defining raw data in order to specify the sample universe. In other words, the steps identified countable observations relevant to the specific study's purposes.

The outcome measure in the study was death within 30 days of admission for a fresh AMI. Death (and survival) within 30 days of this admission were "credited" to the hospital to which the patient with fresh AMI was admitted and not to any other hospital. Reports to individual hospitals accounted for the outcomes of cases that were transferred or readmitted within the 30-day window.

Statistical Manipulation of the Data

After defining the sample universe and the outcome measure, the researchers conducted a series of regression analyses to arrive at the shortest, most informative list of risk factors (that is, those with the greatest probability of making a difference) involved in predicting 30-day death within the sample universe. (Regression analysis is a statistical procedure that results in information on the relative influence of a variety of variables on an outcome variable.) As previously stated, the outcome variable in the AMI study was mortality or survival. The final regression model was able to show which variables in the HCFA data actually have an influence on the outcome, how large the influence is, and whether the influence increases or decreases the likelihood of death.

Tables 9-1 and 9-2 show the AMI study's final risk factors and their beta weights. Beta weights are the values that regression analysis assigns to the variables that the researchers assume will have an influence on the outcome variable. Two separate regression models were built—one for the "no prior admission" sample (table 9-1) and one for the "prior admission" sample (table 9-2). The final risk factors and their beta weights are shown separately for each model. These two samples were separated to add precision in light of the fact that AMI patients with prior admissions were found to experience different types and degrees of risk in comparison to AMI patients with no admission in the prior six months.

In tables 9-1 and 9-2, a beta of 0 indicates a risk factor that has no influence on the likelihood of death for the patient. The more a beta differs from 0, the greater is its influence. Because the outcome variable is death, if a risk factor's beta value is negative, it decreases the likelihood of death; if its beta value is positive, it increases the likelihood of death. In the final computations for the AMI study, the "no prior

Table 9-1. Risk Factors for Patients with No Admission in Prior Six Months

Risk Factor	Beta Value
Age, cutoff at 95, X.054,	
e.g.: Beta for the average age of 75.53 years =	4.067
Pure hypercholesterolemia	− 1.600
Gout, unspecified	− 1.253
Hyperplasia of prostate	− 1.219
Subendocardial infarction	− 1.188
Osteoarthrosis, unspecified whether generalized or localized	− .976
Iron deficiency anemia, unspecified	− .959
Hypothyroidism, unspecified	− .886
Essential hypertension, malignant, benign, or unspecified	− .689
Normocytic anemia due to blood loss	− .649
Obesity	− .564
Aortocoronary bypass status or cardiac pacemaker in situ	− .536
Admitted from skilled nursing facility	.513
Certain malignant neoplasms, but not intrathoracic, intraabdominal, or metastasis (for example, personal	
history of malignant neoplasm of bronchus or lung)	.399
Hypertensive heart disease, unspecified	− .398
Mitral/aortic valve disorders	− 318
Certain disorders of the central nervous system, but not anoxic brain damage (for example, multiple	
sclerosis, epilepsy, cataplexy)	.293
Old myocardial infarction	− .230
Male gender	− .116
Primary diagnosis of AMI of anterolateral wall, other anterior wall, atrium, papillary muscle, or septum alone	.100
Diabetes mellitus, but not in a coma	− .099

Source: Adapted from the Hospital Research and Educational Trust. R. J. Bogue. *Risk-Adjusted 30-Day Mortality of Fresh Acute Myocardial Infarctions: The User's Guide.* Chicago: HRET, 1989.

Table 9-2. Risk Factors for Patients with an Admission in Prior Six Months

Risk Factor	Beta Value
Age, cutoff at 95, X.037,	
e.g.: Beta for average of 75.53 years =	2.795
Current primary Dx of subendocardial infarction	− 1.270
Prior Dx of decubitus ulcer	.835
Prior and current Dx of essential hypertension, malignant, benign, or unspecified	− .813
Current but not prior Dx of essential hypertension, malignant, benign, or unspecified	− .793
Current Dx of unspecified iron deficiency anemia or normocytic anemia due to blood loss	− .742
Admitted from skilled nursing facility	.436
Gout, unspecified; rheumatoid arthritis and other inflammatory polyarthropathies; or osteoarthrosis,	
unspecified whether generalized or localized	− .343
Prior Dx of heart failure	.335
Certain therapeutic and diagnostic operations on the heart or its vessels (for example, aortocoronary	
bypass, angiocardiography, pacemaker in situ, removal of coronary artery obstruction)	− .281
Current Dx of chronic airway obstruction, otherwise unclassified	− .201
Days from last discharge to current admission, X − .022,	
e.g.: Beta for average of 60.07 days =	− .120
Total length of stay, all prior admissions, X.008,	
e.g.: Beta for average of 10.96 days =	.088

Source: Adapted from the Hospital Research and Educational Trust. R. J. Bogue. *Risk-Adjusted 30-Day Mortality of Fresh Acute Myocardial Infarctions: The User's Guide.* Chicago: HRET, 1989.

admission" and the "prior admission" beta weights were applied to their appropriate cases for each hospital, resulting in one prediction about the number of deaths that would be expected for each hospital.

After the influence of each risk factor was determined for all cases, the researchers then applied the risks to each patient at each participating hospital. For example, if a particular hospital had a total of 10 cases of relevant AMIs, each risk factor was applied to each of the 10 cases (for example, age of each patient, whether there was a prior hospital episode in the preceding six months, whether patients were admitted from a skilled nursing facility, and so forth). Then, using the risk factors across all 10 cases at that hospital, the AMI study predicted the number of deaths that should have occurred within 30 days of discharge for these 10 patients. The result was the number of expected deaths within certain categories, as shown in table 9-3. (These results are hypothetical for reasons of confidentiality.) The results of these rather sophisticated data manipulations became the data for the quality assurance (QA), monitoring, and management staff at the hospital.

☐ The Transformation Process

Data collection and manipulation was only a beginning. What were data to the researchers become more or less invisible and uncountable to the QA team at the hospital. Instead, the hospital's QA team found its data in the researchers' results. For this chapter's purpose, this is where the transformation of data into information begins. Table 9-3 shows a hypothetical example of what the researchers' results looked like to the individual hospitals.

A set of specific steps was designed to help the hospital's QA professionals transform these data into useful information. For a checklist of these steps, see figure 9-1.

Step 1. Verify the Data

The first step in the process of using a study's results is to validate the numerical data in order to ensure that the observations being counted—the data—are adequately defined. The individual(s) responsible for this review should work closely with the staff responsible for the data collection, coding, reporting, and analysis in the medical records department. Although this step of matching the results with actual experience (that is, matching data with other available information) will differ from one study to the next, it contributes the first piece of the framework of understanding that will be required in order to extract information from the new results.

In the AMI Study verification of the actual numbers for two groups of Medicare elderly was essential. Both groups would have been diagnosed at the hospital in 1987 as having a fresh AMI. The first group comprised the total number of cases (that is, those Medicare elderly who were admitted and diagnosed as previously described). The second group comprised only those who died. Because the study's results rely on the number of deaths as a function of risk adjustment and on the number and characteristics of an individual hospital's cases, the hospital's quality monitoring and management team would first need to attempt to match the universe of cases in the study with the universe of cases at the hospital.

Because deaths may have occurred following discharge from an individual hospital, it was suggested that the QA team refer to the list of "severe acute heart disease" cases given by HCFA to each hospital as part of the 1987 annual mortality statistics. Most, but not all, of the cases counted as 30-day deaths in the AMI study appeared on the HCFA list. For example, any cases that were transferred out of the hospital may not have appeared on the list for that hospital.

Table 9-3. Risk-Adjusted Outcome Statistics for a Hypothetical Hospital

Variable Describing Cases	Number of Cases	Number of Deaths		Death Rate in Percent		Observed: Expected Deaths	Probability
		Observed	Expected	Observed	Expected		
1. Total number of cases	54	11	15.49	20.4	28.7	0.71	0.115
2. Expected death rate in percent							
Low risk (under 15%)	8	2	0.82	25.0	10.2	4.44	0.194
Medium risk (15 to 29%)	25	6	6.05	24.0	24.2	0.99	0.500
High risk (30% or more)	21	3	8.62	14.3	41.1	0.35	0.012
3. Sex							
Male	23	4	5.66	17.4	24.6	0.71	0.287
Female	31	7	9.83	22.6	31.7	0.71	0.184
4. Age							
65 to 69	12	2	2.14	16.7	17.8	0.94	0.637
70 to 74	12	1	2.80	8.3	23.3	0.36	0.192
75 to 79	17	6	5.29	35.3	31.1	1.14	0.455
80 to 95	13	2	5.27	15.4	40.5	0.38	0.059
5. Any hospital episode in prior six months							
Yes	14	4	4.48	28.6	32.0	0.89	0.518
No	40	7	11.01	17.5	27.5	0.64	0.107
6. Admitted from skilled nursing facility							
Yes	4	2	2.09	50.0	52.2	0.96	0.654
No	50	9	13.41	18.0	26.8	0.67	0.106
7. Reported location of AMI							
Subendocardial	10	4	1.34	40.0	13.4	2.99	0.034
High-risk AMI	11	1	3.20	9.1	29.1	0.31	0.126
Other	33	6	10.96	18.2	33.2	0.55	0.050
8. Hypertension this episode							
Yes	4	1	1.23	25.0	30.7	0.82	0.640
No	50	10	14.27	20.0	28.5	0.70	0.119
9. Diabetes this episode							
Uncomplicated	8	2	2.30	25.0	28.8	0.87	0.582
Complicated	2	0	0.64	0.0	31.8	0.00	0.465
No diabetes	44	9	12.55	20.5	28.5	0.72	0.154
10. Selected heart procedures this episode							
CABG	0	0	0.00	0.0	0.0	1.00	
PTCA	0	0	.00	.0	.0	1.00	
Both	0	0	.00	.0	.0	1.00	
Neither	54	11	15.49	20.4	28.7	0.71	0.115
11. Admission by halves of the year							
1st half	27	5	7.64	18.5	28.3	0.65	0.180
2nd half	27	6	7.85	22.2	29.1	0.76	0.284
12. Admission day of week							
Monday	2	0	0.88	0.0	43.9	0.00	0.315
Tuesday	5	1	1.44	20.0	28.9	0.69	0.552
Wednesday	5	1	1.70	20.0	34.1	0.59	0.446
Thursday	13	0	4.24	0.0	32.7	0.00	0.006
Friday	16	3	4.12	18.8	25.8	0.73	0.378
Saturday	7	4	1.76	57.1	25.2	2.27	0.072
Sunday	6	2	1.34	33.3	22.3	1.49	0.401
13. Admission on							
Weekday	41	5	12.39	12.2	30.2	0.40	0.010
Weekend	13	6	3.10	46.2	23.9	1.93	0.066

Abbreviations: CABG = coronary artery bypass graft; PTCA = percutaneous transluminal coronary angioplasty.

Source: Adapted from the Hospital Research and Educational Trust. R. J. Bogue. *Risk-Adjusted 30-Day Mortality of Fresh Acute Myocardial Infarctions: The User's Guide.* Chicago: HRET, 1989.

Figure 9-1. Checklist for Transforming Data into Information

1. *Verify the data.* Any QA activity that results in new data deserves verification. The means of verifying data will vary greatly from one study to another, but it is always going to be helpful to employ other sources of information to ensure that the data gathered and used in the study accurately represent the number and / or types of patients, procedures, diagnoses, and so on.
2. *Use new data to correct systematic sources of errors in the hospital's data generation system.* A new body of data presents an important opportunity to check the accuracy of, and to correct any problems with, the hospital's information recording, maintenance, and reporting systems.
3. *Narrow the field of interpretation.* It is generally prudent to determine what a body of data does not represent before attempting to specify what it does represent.
4. *Target potential areas for improvement.* The results of a study cannot accomplish all things at once. Seek the opportunities for greatest improvement, or the examples of best performance, and work with them first.
5. *Conduct focused reviews.* No body of data can take the place of focused review, but neither should focused reviews be conducted haphazardly. Step 3 determined what is outside current QA activities, step 4 determined what is inside current QA activities, and step 5 explores the carefully narrowed field of study.
6. *Develop and implement a plan to follow up on medical practices.* Getting people to use the data turns the data into information. The quality monitoring and management staff now know what should be done. They should lead other relevant staff in doing it.
7. *Continue to communicate and report.* Through the process of being transformed into information, each new body of data creates numerous opportunities for integration with ongoing records keeping and reporting for quality management and performance appraisal.

In the AMI study, to identify the deaths that correspond to those reported in the study's results for a given hospital, QA staff would have first acquired a list of all 1987 Medicare admissions with a primary diagnosis of 410 (AMI). Staff would have omitted those patients who were transferred into the hospital and those who were scheduled (elective) admissions. Of those remaining, staff would have then omitted the cases with an AMI in the preceding eight weeks.

It was important to remember that in the QC/MedPAR data set a diagnosis of AMI in the eight weeks prior to the AMI diagnosed at a given hospital would define an AMI as not fresh and that the earlier diagnosis may have been recorded at another institution. Therefore, accurately identifying the correct number of fresh AMIs at a hospital would sometimes require an examination of the AMI patients' medical histories to determine whether some of the patients were treated for an AMI in a different setting during the eight weeks prior to the AMI recorded by this particular hospital.

Even with assistance from the attending physicians, it may not have been possible to arrive at the exact number of observed 30-day deaths subsequent to admission or the total number of cases at a hospital in 1987 with a fresh AMI. But identifying the deaths and cases as accurately as possible was essential to taking further steps to integrate the results of the AMI study into the ongoing QA program. To benefit most from the AMI study, the individual hospitals should have been able to analyze available information about the process of care for the specific group of patients for which the AMI study provided baseline, aggregate, risk-adjusted results.

Step 2. Use New Data to Correct Systematic Sources of Errors in the Hospital's Data Generation System

The question to ask here is, does the hospital's "counting system" work well? In many cases, the data from a particular effort can be checked or verified with other sources of data at the hospital, as in the preceding step. This presents an opportunity to seek out and change systematic problems in how the hospital records, maintains, and reports its data for QA activities.

For example, once all the cases of fresh AMI among Medicare elderly admitted to the institution in 1987 were identified as accurately as possible, the QA staff should have reviewed the discharge abstracts for these cases in light of other available information. If data errors were found, they could then be traced to their sources. Questions to be asked in the AMI study might have included: Are codes being entered incorrectly onto Medicare billing information (for example, heavy use of AMI NOS code 410.9)? Are secondary diagnoses being used appropriately? Because such errors could contribute to a wide variety of problems, such as lower payments or an inadequate medical records review process, it is important to trace the data errors to their source *and* to correct the problem.

In addition, it is possible that a hospital's physicians are providing inadequate documentation for the purposes of accurate and thorough completion of Medicare billing information. It is also possible that abstractors are inconsistently or erroneously coding certain procedures, secondary diagnoses, or other data. In each case, an appropriate corrective action might be to develop educational material. The point here is that being able to compare two sets of overlapping data represents a great opportunity for assessing current data practices. It is equally true that any new data efforts will have better results when a close relationship is maintained between the data collection/analysis processes and the people who will use the data.

Step 3. Narrow the Field of Interpretation

Very early on in the process of integrating new data into an ongoing QA system, it is possible to begin interpreting the data. The first phase of interpretation should probably avoid direct pursuit of quality issues. The reason for this has nothing to do with personal or professional sensitivities. Rather, the process of transforming data into information is representational. The data represent real processes and activities. Hence, it is essential to build a very clear picture of what the data do and do not represent. In other words, this step seeks to narrow the quality monitoring and management team's focus to the data that have the most to say about quality.

In the AMI study, after identifying the fresh AMI cases of Medicare elderly, it was suggested that quality management staff, cardiology medical staff, and other relevant staff be involved in data analysis and review. The aggregate analysis and review at the hospital would focus on identifying and considering the reasons for the hospital's results that were not related to the process of care at the hospital.

The goal of this review of the aggregate data was not to "explain away" the difference between observed and expected numbers of deaths at the institution. Rather, before an accurate and valid assessment of the processes of care could be undertaken, it was necessary to reach a thorough understanding of all the reasons not related to care that might contribute to the difference between observed and expected deaths.

Following are some typical reasons for differences in the number of observed and expected deaths at a given hospital:

- *Imperfect data* due to systematic differences in the data of units, institutions, or time periods. For example, in the AMI study there may have been differences in the criteria used for coding and reporting AMI and the risk-predictor variables by different hospitals and different staff members within each hospital. Such problems can be discovered during data verification.
- *Biased model* due to systematic inaccuracies in the analytic model. For example, in the AMI study there could have been systematic underestimates or overestimates of expected deaths for selected cases or groups of hospitals. Such biases can be checked for after the fact by comparing important groups of cases and repeating steps 1 through 3.
- *Incomplete model* due to the omission of variables that predict the outcome. For example, in the AMI study data on the blood pressure at admission and the elapsed time from the onset of the AMI to hospital admission would have made the analytic model more complete, but were not available. Discovery and consideration of these problems should occur during step 3.

- *Chance variations* typically estimated as a function of the statistical analysis performed. In the AMI study chance variations were estimated and special considerations were developed for results that were based on a small number of expected deaths at an individual hospital and on many comparisons from a large number of hospitals.

The same reasons for statistical differences might be identified for many quality monitoring and management activities.

Also, two specific factors needed to be considered in the AMI study. First, the longer the time from onset of the AMI to admission, the lower the death rate after admission (that is, more patients would have died before being admitted to the hospital). Although prompt admissions of fresh AMIs are advantageous to the patients, they could have been disadvantageous to a hospital's mortality data. Because data on the time of onset of the AMI were not available to the researchers, suitable adjustments could not be made for the higher risk of data associated with prompt admissions. More specifically, fewer AMI patients might have died before admission than during their hospital stay if (1) the patients of a certain hospital were more able or willing to come directly to the hospital's emergency room (ER), (2) local emergency telephone and transportation services were superior, or (3) the hospital's policy favored prompt admission rather than more prolonged care in an ER holding bed. This would have inflated that hospital's actual number of deaths in the AMI study without increasing the study's prediction about the hospital's expected number of deaths and could have made the hospital's performance look worse than it actually was. This point may also have helped to explain why some hospitals did not do as well on weekends (that is, admissions on weekends may typically be faster than they are on weekdays).

Second, a Veterans Administration hospital in the local hospital's area could have meant that previous admissions for some of the hospital's AMIs did not appear in the Medicare data; this could cause the study to predict too few expected deaths. An underprediction of expected deaths would have made the observed number of deaths in the study appear to be too high, when this may not have been the true case.

The key issue here is that the field of focus must be narrowed carefully. If the goal is quality improvement, explanations from areas other than the process of care must be eliminated first. In other words, it helps to know what something is not in order to be more precise about what it is.

Step 4. Target Potential Areas for Improvement

After realistically assessing the effects of other possible reasons for statistical differences, follow-up activities should focus on the process of care at the hospital. It is necessary to remember that the results of any one study cannot take the place of conducting focused reviews. However, the results of one study can play a major role in targeting the review activities. The goal of targeting review activities is to identify areas that appear to be furthest from the standard of 100 percent quality (or provide the best examples of performing near that standard) and hence that permit the greatest movement toward 100 percent quality. For example, in the AMI study there may have been good reasons in a hospital's results to initially focus review activities on certain days of the week or on cases with certain acuity levels (see table 9-3).

The AMI study hospitals might have begun this step by discussing possible explanations for differences between observed and expected deaths with such knowledgeable people as cardiologists, ER physicians, QA staff, and the head analyst for the study. Once alternative explanations for the hospital's results are identified, additional data from the medical record or other sources, such as the ER logs, could be examined to confirm or refine these alternative explanations. For example, in the hypothetical hospital's results from the AMI study, item 2 in table 9-3 shows that the hospital performed poorly for low-risk cases but well for high-risk cases. Because age was the most important risk factor (see tables 9-1 and 9-2), younger patients might not have been treated with an aggressive enough approach. Exploring the ER logs and other medical records might supply information that would verify, refine, or reject this explanation for the hospital's performance with low-risk versus high-risk cases. If a relationship among younger patients, less aggressive treatment, and poor performance appeared to be verified at this step, treatment patterns for younger AMI patients would be a good target for improvement.

Step 5. Conduct Focused Reviews

After identifying the best targets for improvement in the quality of care, the quality management committee should review all, or some of, the medical records of patients whose data make up the sample universe. For example, the subgroup of cases resulting in poor outcomes could be compared to selected cases with positive outcomes in order to identify systematic differences.

As certain areas for improvement were already targeted in step 4, focused reviews may not be necessary for other areas. In the AMI study, for example, step 4 may have identified certain days of the week, certain acuity levels, cases admitted from a skilled nursing facility, or cases with hypertension as the hospital's best target for focused review. It is only prudent to work first where the potential for improvement is greatest.

In the AMI study the decision to review the records of only some cases would depend on the number of AMI admissions (and/or mortalities) the hospital had and the availability of resources. In any study, if only a sample of the records is used, it becomes especially important to include cases (and/or poor outcomes) from each pertinent physician on an equitable basis. In this case, after review and approval by the cardiology medical staff, some set of criteria should be adopted for the focused review.

The sources of information for the review activities in this study could have included the medical records, drug utilization review, pharmacy and therapy review, procedure review, and other sources of information relevant to the treatment of the patients in the study.

Step 6. Develop and Implement a Plan to Follow Up on Medical Practices

By this stage the transformation of data into information is fairly complete. People are beginning to use it. But to ensure maximum and continued use of the information, it is helpful to formalize certain aspects of the data's use by developing and then implementing a follow-up plan. Because of the unique results from any given analysis, as well as the unique relationships that develop in different settings among the administration, the medical staff, and the QA professionals, it is impossible to suggest exactly what that follow-up plan might look like. However, it is important that representatives from each of these groups (administration, medical staff, and quality assurance) be involved in the discussions that lead to such a plan. A clearly documented plan could then develop that will make use of the data and ultimately improve the institution's quality of care.

In the AMI study, with its strong focus on medical outcomes, this step pertained largely to the physicians themselves. The emphasis here was to provide feedback to the physicians involved. The format and manner of distribution for this feedback information should have been developed with assistance from the relevant physicians— the cardiology physicians in the AMI study.

At a minimum, feedback should be provided to the appropriate staff. Often this is, in itself, sufficient follow-up. If it is not, the development of a continuing education program and other follow-up steps with those staff members may be more appropriate. It is important that educational programs or other follow-up steps be developed in cooperation with those whose behavior may require change.

Step 7. Continue to Communicate and Report

It is vital to document all the steps of the follow-up activities. And, for the results of any study to have an impact on the hospital's ongoing quality management program, these documents must be integrated into the ongoing communication and reporting stream.

In the AMI study there were several opportunities for feedback and documentation. For example, the results of the data verification and any corrective actions taken upon discovering problems in data coding and/or reporting should have been used to provide feedback to, develop educational programs for, and evaluate the performance of the medical records department. Similarly, the focused medical records review (stage 5), and any corrective measures taken as a result, should have been documented through feedback to and education of the cardiology staff. Ultimately, communication and reporting activities should provide feedback to all relevant medical staff members, hospital executive managers, and other hospital personnel who can have an influence on the care process for the patients who make up the sample universe for a particular study.

Documents that emerge from the follow-up activities for a study may be placed in the hospital's peer review files, including credentials files, and should be used in reviewing hospital and medical staff bylaws, rules and regulations, and policies and procedures. These documents also should be used in performance appraisal and reappointment and recredentialing processes. Only by integrating the results of the study, and especially the results of the follow-up activities targeted by the study, into the ongoing stream of communications and reports for quality management and performance appraisal activities can the results be expected to pay off in improved quality.

☐ Summary

This chapter set out to guide the reader through the process of transforming data into information. Although the examples provided were particular to one study, and although each effort to extract information from data will differ from the next, certain components of the process were specified as steps that have general application. These steps should enable both the statistician and the nonstatistician to employ a common language in a clear, but thorough process of monitoring and managing the quality of patient care and the accuracy of medical records keeping.